Easy Gardening
for Texas

Jos asabni

E: culturist

Texas A& *tension Service*

TEXAS A&M
AGRILIFE
EXTENSION

CONTRIBUTORS

Patrick Lillard, former Extension Associate, Texas A&M AgriLife
Extension Service; Stephen King, former Associate Professor, Texas A&M
Department of Horticultural Sciences; and Courtney Angel, Nichole Lee,
Ann Boatman, Nathanael Proctor, and Clint Taylor, Graduate Students,
Texas A&M University

Parts of this book were revised and expanded from publications
written by former Extension Horticulturists Charles L. Cole,
Sam Cotner, Frank Dainello, Jerral D. Johnson, Thomas Longbreak,
B. Dean McCraw, Jerry Parsons, and Al Wagner.

Contributors of multiple photographs include: Thomas Isakeit,
Joseph G. Masabni, and Bill Watson, Texas A&M AgriLife Extension Service;
Bart Drees and Jerrold Summerlin, formerly of the Texas A&M AgriLife Extension
Service; Aggie Horticulture (Texas A&M); Scot Nelson, University of Hawai'i
at M noa; Doug Beckers; Bugwood.org; All Is Possible (allispossible.org.uk);
Mark F. Levisay; Julie Steiner (OakleyOriginals); Texas A&M AgriLife Extension
Entomology; U.S. Agricultural Research Service;
U.S. Department of Agriculture; and woodleywonderworks.

*Individual Easy Gardening publications are
available for free download at www.agrilifebookstore.org*

EDITOR
Diane Bowen, Extension Communications Specialist

GRAPHIC DESIGNER
Lori Colvin, Extension Communications Specialist

Texas A&M AgriLife Extension Service

Contents

(continued)

Individual vegetable recommendations

Introduction

If you're new to home gardening, welcome to the satisfaction of producing high-quality foods with peak freshness, flavor, and nutrition. Many gardeners enjoy the hands-on aspects of working in their gardens, knowing how their food is grown, and the savings they see in their food budget.

In fact, home gardening is a popular national pastime. According to the National Garden Association, 35 percent of all households in the United States grow food at home or in a community garden—a 17 percent increase in just 5 years. Much of this increase was among young people ages 18 to 34, households with children, and people living in urban settings.

In *Easy Gardening for Texas,* you'll find information specific to successful gardening in the Lone Star State. In the general garden guidelines, you'll learn growing-season fundamentals—planning your garden; preparing the soil; planting; watering; dealing with diseases, insects, and weeds; and harvesting and storing your produce to enjoy later.

With the help of our individual vegetable recommendations, you can grow many of your favorite garden herbs, and vegetables. Or try something new! Choose what you want to grow and follow the guidelines on what varieties grow best in Texas, plus plenty of tips for planting, growing, and harvesting.

Developed by the small-acreage vegetable specialist of the Texas A&M AgriLife Extension Service, the guidelines in *Easy Gardening for Texas* will help you create a bountiful home garden.

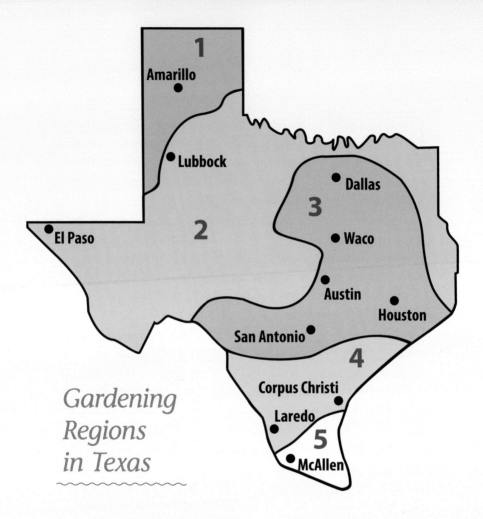

*Gardening
Regions
in Texas*

Texas Gardening Zone	USDA Hardiness Zone	Average minimum temperature
1	6	-10–0°F
2	7	0–10°F
3	8	10–20°F
4	9a	20–25°F
5	9b	25–30°F

General Gardening Guidelines

Source: tillwe (CC BY-SA 2.0)

Source: Ruth and Dave (CC BY 2.0)

Source: National Garden Clubs (CC BY-ND 2.0)

Plan your garden

The first step in establishing a flourishing home vegetable garden is to create a good plan. Planning includes:

- Choosing the garden site
- Deciding on the size of the garden
- Determining the types and varieties of vegetables to plant
- Choosing where, when, and how much of each vegetable to plant in the garden

Source: Lori L. Stalteri (CC BY-2.0)

Successful gardens begin with a good plan.

Select the site

Few people have the perfect garden location, so look for the best spot possible.

Locate the garden where the soil is loose, rich, level, and well drained. Vegetables will not grow in areas where the soil stays wet.

Also, do not plant where weeds do not grow; vegetables will not grow well there either.

Source: Kristine Paulus (CC BY 2.0)

A fire-escape garden

trees or near shrubs; they rob vegetables of food and water.

Plant the garden near a water supply if possible. In many areas, a garden can grow without much additional watering, but it is more likely to be successful if it is irrigated. Water is needed especially during long dry periods and when you plant seeds.

Decide how big to make the garden

Making the garden too large is one of the most common mistakes of enthusiastic, first-time gardeners. A garden that is too large will be too much work. When determining the size, consider these factors:

Vegetables need sunlight to grow well. If possible, avoid areas near buildings, trees, or shrubs that would shade the garden. Most vegetables need at least 8 hours of sunlight daily.

Many types of vegetables are recommended for planting in "full sun." However, in Texas, "full sun" does not mean that they should grow there all day. Here, it's best that they get full sun mostly in the morning, and shade in the heat of the afternoon.

Do not plant vegetables under the branches of large

Space: For apartment dwellers, the garden may be a planter box. A suburban or rural area may have enough garden space.

Time: If the only time you have for gardening is after work or school, or on weekends, there may not be enough time to care for a large garden.

Family size: If gardening is a family activity, a large space can be cared for. A larger family also can use more vegetables.

Reason for gardening: For gardens grown purely for recreation or supplementary food, a container garden or flower bed may be big enough. If you want to can or freeze your vegetables, you'll need a bigger area.

Types of vegetables to be grown: Some vegetables take a lot of room. Most need at least 3 feet of space between rows. If you want to plant 10 rows of vegetables, the garden must be at least 30 feet wide.

Choose what to grow

What to grow in the garden is as big a decision as where to locate it. Consider the following points in selecting vegetables:

Space: Watermelons need too much room for small gardens. Other vine crops such as cucumbers and cantaloupes can fit in a small garden if they are trained on a fence, trellis, or other structure.

Vegetables that can be

Plant tall vegetables where they won't shade shorter plants.

grown in small gardens include beans, beets, broccoli, cabbage, carrots, eggplants, greens, onions, peppers, radishes, and bush squash.

Light: Most vegetables need 8 hours of sun. Those that can be grown in shaded areas include beets, broccoli, cabbage, carrots, cauliflower, and greens.

Expected production: The smaller the garden, the more important it is to get high production from each row.

Small, fast-maturing crops such as radishes, turnips, and beets yield quickly and need little space. Beans, squash, and tomatoes require more space but produce over a long season.

Cost of vegetables if bought: Plant vegetables that are expensive to buy. Broccoli is usually one of the more expensive vegetables that can be grown in most home gardens.

Food value: All vegetables are good, but some are more nutritious than others. Grow different kinds of vegetables to put more variety in your diet.

Personal preference: This is especially important if the garden is purely for recreation or personal enjoyment. Grow vegetables your family likes to eat.

Arrange plants by height and harvest time

Design your garden to use space and light efficiently. Group tall vegetables such as okra, corn, and tomatoes together on the north side of the garden where they won't shade shorter vegetables such as bush beans.

Also, group vegetables according to maturity. For example, you could plant and harvest an early crop such as lettuce or beets, and then plant peppers in their place. See page 9 for other ideas on what to grow first.

Plant small, fast-maturing vegetables between larger ones.

Source: Doug Beckers (CC BY-SA 2.0)

Snow peas trained on a bamboo and rope trellis

If possible, plant vine crops near a fence or trellis.

Make a drawing on paper to show the location and spacing of vegetables in your garden.

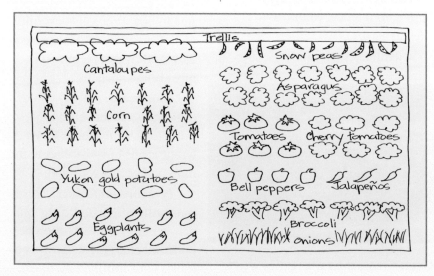

A garden plan

Plant at the right time

Vegetables fall into two general groups—warm season and cool season.

Warm-season crops cannot tolerate frost and will not grow when the soil is cool. They include beans, corn, cucumbers, eggplants, okra, peppers, squash, and tomatoes.

Plant them after the last frost in the spring, and early enough to mature before frost in the fall.

Cool-season crops can stand lower temperatures; plant them before the soil warms in the spring. They include beets, broccoli, cabbage, carrots, greens, onions, and radishes.

They also can be planted in late summer to harvest after the first killing (or hard) frost in the fall.

Determine how much to plant

The amount to plant depends on several factors, including your household size, the amount of vegetables that the plant can produce, and your plans for preserving or giving away some of your harvest.

Do not plant too much. Over-planting requires too much work.

Approximate amount to plant per person for fresh use

Beets	10 feet
Broccoli	4 plants
Carrots	10 feet
Corn	15 feet
Cucumbers	2 hills
Green beans, bush	15 feet
Green beans, pole	5 feet
Greens	10 feet
Lettuce, leaf	10 feet
Okra	6 feet
Onions	5 feet
Peppers	3 plants
Radishes	5 feet
Squash, summer	2 hills
Tomatoes	3 plants

Source: Bill Watson

Prep the soil

The soil is a storehouse for most of what plants need to grow: nutrients, organic matter, air, and water. It also provides support for their roots.

If you prepare and tend to the soil properly, you can improve it each year, and it can continue to grow plants forever. Neglected soil soon becomes suitable only for weeds.

Know your soil type and condition

Texas gardeners must work with many different types of soils—including compacted clays, loose sands, and shallow, chalky soils.

Sandy soils do not hold enough water; in windy areas, blowing sand can injure the vegetables. Clay soils can hold too much water and prevent enough air from entering the soil.

Vegetables need a deep, well-drained soil with

Source: cogdogblog (CC BY 2.0)

Take soil samples from several areas of the garden and mix them together.

adequate organic matter—material from once-living organisms, such as leaves or grass clippings. Good garden soil with proper moisture will not form a hard ball when squeezed in your hand. It should crumble easily when forced between the fingers. It should not crack or crust over when dry.

Test the soil

Have the soil in a new garden tested every year for the first 3 years, and then every 2 to 3 years afterward. This is especially important for beginning gardeners who are unfamiliar with growing vegetables.

A soil test will tell you how much of each nutrient is in the soil and how much to add. The results can save you time and money on additives that aren't needed. They can also indicate how your activities are affecting your soil's health over time.

To collect a soil sample:

1. Choose a time when the soil is moist but not wet.
2. Dig down about 4 to 6 inches and take a handful of soil. Sample several places in the garden.
3. Place each handful of soil in a large container and mix it.
4. From this mixture, use about 1 quart of soil for the sample.
5. Send the sample and a completed form to a laboratory for testing. The Texas A&M AgriLife Extension Soil, Water and Forage Testing Laboratory (http://soiltesting.tamu.edu/) offers soil testing services, as do several private companies.

For spring planting, have the soil tested in midwinter. County Extension agents (htpp://counties.agrilife.org) can give you a soil sample container and explain where to send the sample for testing.

Improve the soil

Almost all garden soils can be improved by adding organic matter to make the soil more workable. Organic matter:

- Loosens tight clay
- Helps sand hold more water
- Makes soil easier to dig
- Adds nutrients

Some common organic additives are:

- **Compost:** Compost consists of decayed plant

11

Source: cogdogblog (CC BY 2.0)

Compost consists of organic matter such as decayed leaves and grass clippings.

materials. Work it into the soil before planting.

- *Green manure:* Plant rye or oats in the fall and spade or plow it under in the spring. These cannot be used if you will plant a fall garden. For a fall garden, plant southern peas in the summer about 10 days before planting.

- *Manure:* Use composted manure and incorporate it into the soil well ahead of planting. Do not use fresh manure, as it can damage plants and introduce diseases. Apply 30 to 40 pounds of composted manure for every 100 square feet.

- *Sawdust:* Compost this before adding it to the garden. Do not use uncomposted sawdust because it will rob the soil

of nitrogen and, consequently, starve the plants of this essential nutrient.

Add plant materials

Work leaves, straw, and grass clippings into the soil several months before planting to allow it time to decompose. Most gardeners do this during the winter. Do not add more than a 4-inch-deep layer of organic material.

Most heavy clay soils benefit from the addition of gypsum. Although it adds some nutrients, it more importantly loosens the soil and makes it more workable.

If your soil is heavy clay, spread about 3 to 4 pounds of gypsum (available at nurseries and garden centers) per 100 square feet over the garden soil after it has been dug in the winter. Work it into the soil or allow it to be washed in by rain.

You could also add sand and organic matter to clay soil to make it more workable. Mix 2 inches of clean sand and 3 inches of organic matter, such as leaves, into the soil.

Till the soil

Till the soil as deeply as possible, at least 8 to 10 inches.

Source: Bill Watson

A well-prepared garden is free of sticks, rocks, and other material.

Deep tilling loosens the soil and enables the vegetable roots to go deeper. Completely turn over the soil to a depth of 8 to 12 inches, using a spade or rototiller.

Till the soil when it is moist but not wet. Working soil when it is too wet can cause it to become rough.

For spring planting, spade the soil in the winter. Winter temperatures and moisture will help mellow the soil. This is especially important if you are working the soil for the first time.

To build and maintain the soil, add organic matter during soil preparation each year. Be sure that all plant material is turned under the soil.

If you add organic material before planting a fall garden, make sure that it is well rotted, such as compost.

Before planting, rake the soil clean and level it. Remove the sticks, rocks, and other material.

Prepare the rows

In most of Texas, vegetables grow best on raised beds, which:

- Allow water to drain away from the roots
- Provide furrows for irrigation
- Allow air to enter soil
- Help plants survive rainy periods

If the garden is large enough, space the rows 3 feet apart. Where space is a problem, you could plant some vegetables in closer rows. However, they will require more care during the growing season.

Source: Ruth and Dave (CC BY 2.0)

Raised beds can improve drainage and aeration for vegetables.

13

Straight beds are nice but not necessary. They are not as important for small gardens that you work with a hoe, rake, or other hand tools. If your garden is large and you work it with a rototiller or garden tractor, make the rows as straight as possible.

Use a shovel or rake to pull the soil up into beds 8 to 10 inches high. Tamp down the beds or allow them to settle before planting.

Also, level the tops of the beds and widen them to about 6 to 8 inches before planting. You will plant on top of the beds.

As you prepare the soil for planting, gardening might seem anything but "easy." But with good soil preparation, gardening will become easier every year.

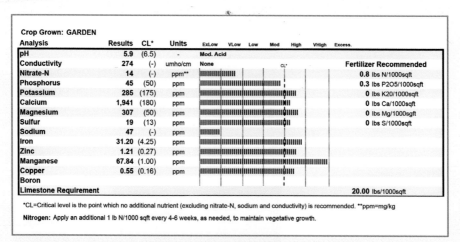

Crop Grown: GARDEN

Analysis	Results	CL*	Units	ExLow	VLow	Low	Mod	High	VHigh	Excess.	
pH	5.9	(6.5)	-	Mod. Acid							
Conductivity	274	(-)	umho/cm	None			CL*				Fertilizer Recommended
Nitrate-N	14	(-)	ppm**	‖‖‖‖‖‖‖‖‖‖							0.8 lbs N/1000sqft
Phosphorus	45	(50)	ppm	‖‖‖‖‖‖‖‖‖‖‖‖‖‖‖‖‖‖							0.3 lbs P2O5/1000sqft
Potassium	285	(175)	ppm	‖‖‖‖‖‖‖‖‖‖‖‖‖‖‖‖‖‖							0 lbs K2O/1000sqft
Calcium	1,941	(180)	ppm	‖‖‖‖‖‖‖‖‖‖‖‖‖‖‖‖‖‖							0 lbs Ca/1000sqft
Magnesium	307	(50)	ppm	‖‖‖‖‖‖‖‖‖‖‖‖‖‖‖‖‖‖							0 lbs Mg/1000sqft
Sulfur	19	(13)	ppm	‖‖‖‖‖‖‖‖‖‖‖‖‖‖‖‖‖‖							0 lbs S/1000sqft
Sodium	47	(-)	ppm	‖‖‖‖‖‖‖							
Iron	31.20	(4.25)	ppm	‖‖‖‖‖‖‖‖‖‖‖‖‖‖‖‖‖‖							
Zinc	1.21	(0.27)	ppm	‖‖‖‖‖‖‖‖‖‖‖‖‖‖‖‖‖‖							
Manganese	67.84	(1.00)	ppm	‖‖‖‖‖‖‖‖‖‖‖‖‖‖‖‖‖‖‖‖‖‖‖							
Copper	0.55	(0.16)	ppm	‖‖‖‖‖‖‖‖‖‖‖‖‖‖‖‖‖							
Boron											
Limestone Requirement											20.00 lbs/1000sqft

*CL=Critical level is the point which no additional nutrient (excluding nitrate-N, sodium and conductivity) is recommended. **ppm=mg/kg

Nitrogen: Apply an additional 1 lb N/1000 sqft every 4-6 weeks, as needed, to maintain vegetative growth.

An example of soil test results and fertilizer recommendations from the Texas A&M AgriLife Extension Service Soil, Water and Forage Testing Laboratory

Plant

One of the most enjoyable phases of gardening is planting. Because planting is easy, almost everyone can participate. Gardeners enjoy watching the seeds they planted sprout and begin to grow.

Below are general recommendations on seeds, transplants, and tools for your home garden. Guidelines for planting specific types of vegetables are included in the "Individual Plant Recommendations" section.

Seeds

Buy seeds early to leave time to order varieties that might not be available locally. Most seed companies will send catalogs of vegetable types and varieties on request. Refer to your garden plan to see how much of each vegetable to plant.

Don't order more seeds than you need for this year's spring and fall gardens. Although you could save most seeds to use next year if you stored them properly, it is usually best to get new seeds at least every 2 years.

Transplants are usually better for growing some crops, including tomatoes.

Transplants

Many crops do better if you start them indoors and then transplant them into the garden. Transplants are usually best for growing broccoli, cauliflower, peppers, eggplants, and tomatoes.

Home gardeners can buy or grow their own transplants. If you decide to buy them, choose healthy plants that are free of insects and diseases.

Harden homegrown transplants before planting them in the garden. To harden your transplants, follow these steps about 10 days before transplanting:

- Reduce watering, but do not allow the plants to wilt.
- Gradually expose the plants to garden conditions by placing them outside in a protected spot.
- Do not fertilize before transplanting.
- Do not over-harden the plants, as this will stunt their growth.

Purchased transplants may already be hardened when you buy them. If you are unsure, ask the nursery for advice.

Tools

The planting equipment you will need depends on the size of the garden. In most home gardens, a hoe, rake, hand trowel, string, stakes, and labels are sufficient.

In large gardens, a hand planter, rototiller, or garden tractor may be useful.

Rototillers can be useful in large gardens, and they are usually available for rent if you don't own one.

Timing

Texas has five gardening regions. When making planting decisions, refer to the garden regions map on page 2 to compare the temperature extremes in your area to those of the USDA Plant Hardiness Zone Map for Texas on pages 219–220.

Cool-season crops are best suited for fall harvest. They are usually planted in September when the weather starts to cool.

You might be able to plant cool-season crops such as broccoli and lettuce as soon as you can work the soil in the spring. If you plant too late, hot weather will reduce both the size and quality of your harvest.

Wait to plant warm-season crops such as beans and tomatoes until the soil has warmed. These crops grow poorly or not at all when the soil temperature is below 65°F. For fall gardens, plant warm-season crops early enough to mature before the first frost.

Seeding

Plant the seeds when the soil is moist but not wet. If you work wet soil, it may crust over and prevent the seedlings from breaking through.

To make the rows straight, stretch a string between two stakes to use as a guide. If you plant in straight rows, you will be less likely to cut off a plant accidentally during hoeing and will be better able to distinguish vegetables from weeds in the seedling stage. Use a hoe handle, narrow stick, or a similar tool to make a seeding trench along the string.

Do not plant the seeds too deep:

- **Small seeds** such as carrots, greens, radishes, and lettuce: ¼ to ½ inch deep
- **Medium-sized seeds** such as beets and okra: ½ to 1 inch deep
- **Large seeds** such as beans, corn, and squash: 1 to 1½ inches deep

To get a good stand, plant

Source: Daniel Gasteiger (CC BY 2.0)

Bean seeds are considered large sized, and should be planted 1½ inches deep.

Source: Doug Beckers (CC BY-SA 2.0)

Mustard greens seedlings—before thinning (left), and after

more seeds than you need and thin the plants after they have come up to get the proper spacing. This is especially important if you use old seeds. Thin the plants while they are still small to avoid damaging them.

Seedlings that aren't thinned will be crowded and will not grow or yield as well as they would have with enough room.

Transplanting

If you're setting out plants rather than sowing seeds, the timing will differ. For spring, plant transplants later than you would seeds; for fall crops, plant transplants earlier than seeds.

The ideal time to transplant is as soon as the soil dries after a rain. Transplant on a cloudy day or late in the afternoon. This gives the plants time to recover from transplanting before they are exposed to the sun.

1. Before planting, water the transplants thoroughly.

2. Using a hoe or trowel, make holes deep enough in the row so you can set the plants slightly deeper than where they grew in the pots.

3. Make a starter solution by dissolving 2 tablespoons of garden fertilizer, such as 10-10-10, in 1 gallon of water.

4. Fill the hole with the starter solution and allow it to soak into the soil.

5. Remove the transplant from the pot or tray.

6. Set the transplant in the hole.

7. Firm the soil around the roots. Leave a dish-shaped depression around the plant to hold water.

8. Water it well to make

Source: Joseph G. Masabni

Clear plastic sheeting used as a row cover

Source: AmberStrocel (CC BY-ND 2.0)

Row cover protecting spinach

sure the soil is in good contact with the roots.

When setting out plants growing in peat pots, cover all of the pot with soil. Peat pots exposed to the air draw moisture away from the plant roots. You may need to cover eggplant, pepper, and tomato plants to protect them from late spring frosts.

Frost and sun protection

Be prepared to protect your plants each time freezing weather is expected. Cover the plants with straw, row covers, frost blankets or another type of frost protection. Remove the protection as soon as the danger of frost is past.

Plants set in the garden in late summer for a fall garden will need some protection from the sun. A shingle, piece of cardboard, or similar object placed on the west side of the plant will provide shade.

Source: Joseph G. Masabni

Fabric used to protect young plants from frost

Fertilize

Of the 16 nutrient elements that plants need, the three most abundant—carbon, hydrogen, and oxygen—come from water and the air. The other nutrients come from the soil. You can add nutrients via compost, fertilizers, or manure.

If your plants are not growing well, fertilizing them will help only if a lack of nutrients is causing the problem. Fertilizer will not help plants that are growing in poorly drained soils, under too much shade, or in competition with weeds or tree roots.

Test the soil

For specific guidelines on what your soil does and does not need, have it tested by an accredited laboratory (see page 11). Otherwise, you could waste money and do more harm than good.

For example, if you apply too much nitrogen to fruit crops such as cucumbers, squash, or tomatoes, the plants may produce all vines but no fruit. Or if you add unnecessary phosphorus, it could kill the fungi that the plants need to absorb iron, resulting in an iron deficiency and poor production.

Decide what kind of fertilizer to use

Fertilizers fall into two general categories: organic and inorganic.

Organic fertilizers are made of materials from a living or once-living animal or plant. They include bone meal, cottonseed meal, fish meal, manure (cow, horse, or poultry), peat moss, worm castings, or other naturally occurring materials.

Inorganic, or chemical, fertilizers are manufactured products. Examples are ammonium chloride, ammonium nitrate, ammonium phosphate, ammonium sulfate, and urea.

Advantages of organic fertilizers

- Organic fertilizers not only provide nutrients, they also improve the soil's structure and ability to hold water and nutrients. Over time, they can make your soil and plants healthier.

- Because organic fertilizers release nutrients slowly, you're unlikely to over fertilize and damage your plants or the environment.
- Organic fertilizers are biodegradable and environmentally friendly.

Disadvantages of organic fertilizers

- Because organic fertilizers rely on microorganisms to break down and release nutrients into the soil, they work more slowly than do chemical fertilizers.
- You often won't know the exact nutrient content of an organic fertilizer.
- Purchased organic fertilizer is more expensive than inorganic fertilizers because you need more of it to get the same amount of nutrients.

Source: Ragesoss (CC BY-SA 3.0)

Peat moss

Source: John D. Byrd, Mississippi State University, Bugwood.org

Fertilizer burn on corn caused by adding too much chemical fertilizer

Advantages of chemical fertilizers

- Plants can use the nutrients from a chemical fertilizer immediately.
- You can buy exactly the ratio of nutrients that your plants need.

Disadvantages of chemical fertilizers

- Although chemical fertilizers help plants grow, they do not improve the soil.
- They are made primarily of nonrenewable sources such as petrochemicals.
- It's easy to over-fertilize and injure or kill the plants.
- Chemical fertilizer seeps easily into water supplies to pollute creeks, lakes, rivers, and drinking water.

Understand the fertilizer analysis

The three numbers on inorganic fertilizer containers are the *fertilizer analysis*.

They indicate the percentage of nitrogen, phosphorus, and potassium in the fertilizer. These figures are always listed in the same order.

For example, a 100-pound bag of 10-20-10 fertilizer contains 10 pounds of nitrogen, 20 pounds of phosphorus, and 10 pounds of potassium. This equals a total of 40 pounds of nutrients.

The rest of the product, or 60 pounds in this example, is a carrier or filler such as sand,

Source: Bill Watson

A bag containing 13 percent nitrogen, 13 percent phosphorus, and 13 percent potassium (or potash)

Cauliflower leaves showing symptoms of a nitrogen deficiency

Corn plants that are deficient in phosphorus

Tomato leaf showing signs of a potassium deficiency

perlite, or rice hulls. A complete fertilizer is one that includes all three elements.

Nitrogen: All parts of a plant need nitrogen to grow—the roots, leaves, stems, flowers, and fruit. Nitrogen gives plants their green color and is used to form protein.

A lack of nitrogen causes the lower leaves to turn yellow and the whole plant to turn pale green. For example, it can cause poor ear production in corn. On the other hand, too much nitrogen kills plants.

Phosphorus enables cells to divide and helps form roots, flowers, and fruit. A phosphorus deficiency causes stunted growth and poor flowering and fruiting.

Potassium: Plants need potassium for many of the chemical processes that allow them to live and grow. Although potassium shortages show up in various ways, common symptoms in many plants are stunted growth and yellowish lower leaves.

If you have not had your garden soil tested, use 2 to 3 pounds of a complete fertilizer such as 10-20-10 for every 100 square feet of garden area.

For example, a 10 × 10 foot plot (or 5 × 20 foot) would be 100 square feet. A garden that is 30 feet long with rows 3 feet apart would have rows almost 100 square feet long. For that size of garden, you would use 2 pounds of fertilizer if the garden is sandy and 3 pounds if the soil is mostly clay.

Do not use too much chemical fertilizer. It can kill plants, pollute the environment, and torpedo your harvest. If it doesn't kill them, you may get huge plants, but they won't set flowers or bear fruit.

Never use fresh manure as fertilizer because it can injure your plants, contaminate the vegetables, and give people potentially fatal diseases.

Choose the fertilizer

When you buy fertilizer, consider the cost per pound of the nutrient(s). Generally, the higher-analysis fertilizers and larger containers are less expensive.

For example, a 50-pound bag of 10-20-10 may not cost any more than a 50-pound bag of 5-10-5 fertilizer, but the 10-20-10 bag contains twice the nutrients.

If you choose a starter fertilizer, look for one with twice as much phosphorus as nitrogen or potassium. An example would be 10-20-10 or 12-24-12. A good general purpose garden fertilizer is 15-5-10.

Do not use lawn fertilizers on a vegetable garden. They contain too much nitrogen, and they may include chemicals for lawn weed control that can injure or kill your vegetables.

Source: Doug Beckers (CC BY-SA 2.0)

Organic fertilizer is available commercially in pellet form.

Soils with pH levels below 5.7 need lime. Lime adds calcium to the soil and makes it less acidic, raising the pH to an acceptable level.

Apply the fertilizer

Fertilizers are applied four ways:

- **Broadcast before planting:** Before you make the rows, spread the proper amount of fertilizer evenly over the garden and mix it with the soil to a depth of 3 to 4 inches. This method is the least likely to damage the plants and usually is best for home gardeners.

- **Band or row applications:** Apply the fertilizer in a strip along the side of the row before planting. Take care to prevent the roots from coming in contact with the fertilizer band, which can kill the plants.

- **Starter solution:** Use starter solution only on transplants such as cabbage, eggplants, peppers, and tomatoes. Mix 2 tablespoons of garden fertilizer in 1 gallon of water and stir well. Pour 1 cup of the mix into the hole and let it soak in before transplanting.

- **Application to growing plants (side-dressing):** Sprinkle fertilizer along the sides of rows and water it into the soil.

- **Incorporation into the soil:** If you are using organic fertilizer such as composted barnyard manure, spread it evenly over the garden and work it into the soil.

Because organic fertilizers need time to break down their nutrients and make them available to the plants, apply them a few months before planting. An exception is a liquid organic fertilizer such as fish emulsion, which can be applied at planting or during the growing season.

About ½ cup of garden fertilizer for every 10 feet of row usually is enough. The amount and timing of fertilizer needed varies according to the type of vegetable planted.

For most vegetables, side-dressing increases the harvest. It is especially helpful on sandy soils or where heavy rains may have leached nutrients from the soil.

Fertilize fall gardens in the same way as for spring gardens. If you plant a fall garden after a well-fertilized spring garden, you'll need only about half the spring fertilizer rate at planting.

Water

A critical part of vegetable gardening is determining the right amount of water to give them. Watering too much, too little, or at the wrong time can leave your plants susceptible to diseases and reduce your harvest.

Water at the right time

Instead of watering "every 3 days" or "once a week," keep an eye on both the plants and the soil—let them tell you when you need to water.

Plants: Don't water plants that are drowning. Common symptoms of too much water are wilted plants, brown young leaves, yellow lower leaves, rotting or stunted roots, and slower growth.

Signs of too little water include wilted plants, yellowing leaves, dried leaves toward the bottom of the plant, and roots beginning to appear at the surface. Water the plants before they reach this point.

Soil: Cracked ground and powdery soil are too dry and need watering. If the soil is greenish, it usually means that algae are growing there, indicating that the soil is too wet.

Give your plants enough water to keep the soil moist but not wet in the root zone. To determine when to water, squeeze a handful of soil. If it's sticky or water drips out, it doesn't need water. If the soil is crumbly, it's time to water.

An excellent tool for determining if the garden needs water is a soil moisture probe or sensor. These probes are available at garden centers for $10 to $50, depending on the model. A mid-range price will usually get you a quality tool that gives accurate information such as % *soil moisture*, instead of general information such as *wet* or *dry*.

If possible, water in the morning. Diseases are more likely to crop up if you water at night because they develop fastest in cool, moist conditions.

For the same reason, try not to spray water on the leaves.

Plants need water throughout the growing season: If the soil fluctuates from flooded to bone dry, you'll get a smaller, lower-quality harvest than if it stays more uniformly moist.

Water more often when the seeds are just planted to keep the soil moist and prevent surface crusting.

As the plant grows, water less often but more deeply to enable the water to penetrate through the root zone.

Add mulch to keep the moisture in the soil and to reduce evaporation loss. If you use chemical fertilizers, always water them into the soil immediately after application. Fertilizers are salts that can draw

Source: Sean Loyless (CC BY 2.0)
Cracked, powdery soil is too dry.

water out of the plant tissues, causing them to burn.

Methods

The most efficient way to water vegetables is via drip irrigation, which places water where it is needed.

Two types of drip irrigation products are commonly available for home gardeners:

• **Drip tape** is sold at most garden supply stores; a typical 4-foot-wide raised bed needs at least three drip lines. Manage the drip system to prevent the water from flowing off the bed shoulder.

Drip tape also can blow off beds in windy weather; to avoid this, bury the tape under a shallow layer of soil—2 to 4 inches—depending on what vegetables you are growing.

• **Drip tubing**, such as a soaker hose, is often laid along side rows of vegetable plants, but it also can be used to supply water under plastic mulches.

Although tubing lines can also be buried, in some areas they can be damaged by rodents and ants.

To reduce clogging, always bury the lines with the emitter opening facing up.

For more detailed information about watering your garden, see *Easy Gardening: Watering Your Vegetables*, which is available for free download at http://www.agrilifebookstore.org.

Source: davetrainer (CC BY-SA 2.0)

Drip irrigation tape

Source: USDAgov (CC BY 2.0)

A drip tubing irrigation line along a row of berry bushes

Mulch

One of the gardener's best friends is mulch. Mulch is a layer of material such as straw, bark, compost, or plastic that is placed around plants to provide a variety of benefits.

Mulch can help you:

- Conserve water by enabling the soil to soak up more water and reducing evaporation from the soil
- Reduce weeding by blocking light from emerging weed seedlings. A 4-inch layer of mulch on the soil surface keeps most annual weed seedlings from coming through.
- Protect against disease by keeping vegetables such as tomatoes and eggplants off the ground and by preventing raindrops from splashing disease organisms from the soil onto the plants
- Protect the roots from heat or cold:
    - ❖ In early spring, soil under plastic or dark organic

Source: martindelisle31 (CC BY-SA 2.0)

A melon protected by straw mulch

mulch warms faster than does bare soil, which enables you to plant warm-season crops earlier.

❖ In the summer, mulch helps keep the soil cooler. To do this, use light-colored paper such as newspaper or sawdust.

❖ Applied in late fall, winter mulch insulates the roots, crowns, and stems of winter crops from extreme cold.

- **Reduce erosion,** especially in sloping gardens.

- **Increase harvest** by enabling the rows to be spaced more closely. A well-mulched garden can yield 50 percent more vegetables than can an unmulched garden of the same size.

- **Improve the soil,** if you use organic mulch, by gradually making the soil more fertile.

Choose the mulch

When choosing mulch, consider these factors:

- **The type of vegetable you plan to mulch:** Never mulch with material from the crop that you want to use it on. For example, do not use potato vines from the spring crop to mulch fall potatoes. This increases the possibility of transmitting diseases to the new crop.

- **The season when the mulch will be used:** Use light-colored mulch in the summer and early fall to reflect heat. Use dark-colored mulch in early spring to help warm the soil to permit earlier planting and speed early growth.

Mulches are classified as inorganic or organic. Inorganic mulches include plastic, rocks, and other nonplant materials.

Source: Joseph G. Masabni

Newspaper used as mulch

The only inorganic mulch used in vegetable gardens is plastic.

At the end of the season, organic mulch such as straw or newspaper can be turned under the soil to enable it to break down before you replant the garden.

Many common materials are used as mulch in vegetable gardens:

Compost is generally the best mulch material for home gardens. It is inexpensive and usually has no weed seeds. To save more money, you also could prepare compost from materials already in your yard.

If you buy it from a source such as a city composting service, make sure that the materials it is made of do not include heavy metals or other harmful matter.

Newspapers make a good base for other organic mulches. Apply them shredded or up to eight sheets thick; then cover them with another mulch to keep them from blowing away.

Because newspapers are printed with soy-based inks, they are safe to use in vegetable gardens. Do not use glossy magazines because their inks can

Source: woodleywonderworks (CC BY-SA 2.0)

Black plastic and straw used as a weed barrier

Source: stellar678 (CC BY-SA 2.0) Source: bnpositive (CC BY-SA 2.0) Source: Carlin Joe (CC BY 2.0)

Straw, grass clippings, and pine needles are all good organic mulches.

contain heavy metals or other contaminants.

Sawdust, managed well, can be good mulch. However, it can also reduce soil nitrogen temporarily.

To avoid this problem, add nitrogen to the sawdust and then compost it before spreading it on your garden.

Straw is coarse and short-lived. You'll need more straw to get the same effect as from compost or lawn clippings.

Plastic can be an effective mulch if used properly. Use black plastic in the spring and early summer to warm the soil. Black plastic keeps light from the soil and prevents weeds from growing. Clear plastic warms the soil, but weeds can grow beneath the plastic.

A disadvantage of plastic is that you cannot mix it into the soil at season's end.

Other organic materials that would make good mulch include bark, buckwheat hulls, cocoa-bean hulls, coffee grounds, crushed corncobs, spent hops, leaves, mushroom compost, peanut hulls, pecan shells, pine needles, and wood chips.

Spread the mulch

Spread mulch on freshly cultivated, weed-free soil before the vegetable plants are large enough to interfere. Apply organic mulch thick enough to leave a 4-inch layer after settling.

If the material is fine textured, a layer 4 inches deep should be enough.

However, because coffee

Source: rfduck (CC BY-ND 2.0)　　Source: Jessica M. Cross (CC BY 2.0)　　Source: USDAgov

Bark and wood chips are also organic. Plastic is the only inorganic mulch.

grounds have a very fine texture and become compacted easily, thick layers of them can inhibit the movement of moisture and air. Instead of using only coffee grounds, apply about a half-inch layer of coffee grounds and cover it with about a 4-inch layer of coarse organic mulch such as wood chips.

Coarser materials, such as straw, will settle and may require 8 inches or more initially.

If you use organic materials, add more mulch during the season. During the growing season, the mulch settles and gradually rots at the point where it meets the moist soil surface.

Save money

A bag of mulch from the store doesn't go very far. But there's no need to buy mulch when suitable materials are available at little or no cost. Check out these possible sources of free or inexpensive mulch:

- For shredded tree trimmings, call your electric company, phone company, tree services, landscaping companies, city parks or street maintenance department—some may dump them at your house for free. However, keep an eye out for poison ivy and other rash-inducing plants. And wear sturdy gloves to avoid splinters.
- Seasonal mulch can come in the form of shredded Christmas trees. Or, in the fall, ask local businesses if they

will donate the bales of hay they used in their fall displays.

- If your area has industries like food processing, you can often get waste products for free. Companies, especially smaller ones, are often glad to give you their leftovers.
- For manure that you could compost for mulch, try local stables, a dairy farm, or a poultry farm.
- Ask a local microbrewer for spent hops and grain.
- Cruise curbsides for bags of leaves and grass clippings. Sunday evenings are good times to look; many people mow or rake leaves on the weekend and set out bags of them at the curb on Sundays.

- Offer to rake and bag pine needles from a neighbor's backyard—your neighbor gets free "lawn service," and you get free mulch.
- Local garden centers may offer discounts on torn bags of soil and mulch, especially on Mondays.
- Many coffee shops give away used coffee grounds.
- Send a request for mulch on Freecycle (https://www.freecycle.org/).
- For other local sources, contact your county Extension agent or the local newspaper's garden writer.

If you plan to get a lot of mulch, buy a pitchfork. It makes the work much easier.

Source: Cara Harpole (CC BY 2.0)

Compost

If we composted many of the materials that we throw away—such as leaves, grass clippings, and kitchen scraps—we could divert and make use of 20 to 30 percent of the trash currently going into landfills. By composting these materials, we can reduce the amount of waste we generate as well as produce organic matter and nutrients for our gardens and yards.

Source: Katie Teague, uacescomm (CC BY-SA 2.0)

Garden-ready compost

Composting is simply the breakdown of organic matter. The resulting substance is called compost.

Every garden can benefit from the addition of compost because it supplies many of the nutrients that plants need. Compost also helps aerate the soil and enables it to hold water and nutrients better.

Set up the pile

Although many types of composting bins are available for sale, they can easily be made with bricks, cement blocks, scrap lumber, wire fencing, or wooden pallets.

Enclosing the pile uses less space, but you could leave it freestanding if you have enough room. If you enclose the pile, leave an opening on one side so you can turn the compost with a fork to allow air to enter the pile.

Set up the compost pile in an area that is:

- Secluded
- Preferably near the garden
- Partially shaded to prevent the pile from drying out too fast
- Well drained so it does not become waterlogged

If you have room, you could make three compost piles—one that's ready to use, one being turned, and one being filled up.

Add the right materials

To decompose properly, a compost heap must have four

Source: Joi (CC BY 2.0)

A compost bin placed in a secluded spot near the garden, and in partial shade

elements: organic material, microorganisms (also called microbes), air, and water.

Microbes do the work of breaking down organic materials into compost. To survive, they need air, water, and nitrogen. The only one of these that you can't add too much of is air.

Many types of organic materials can be used in compost piles:

- **Kitchen scraps:** Coffee grounds and filters, eggshells, and fruit and vegetable trimmings are great items for the compost pile. Do not use animal products such as fat, grease, dairy products, or meat trimmings because they break down slowly, attract rodents and other pests, and smell bad when they decompose.

- **Grass clippings:** Grass clippings have relatively high nitrogen content and make good compost. Mix green, fresh clippings with soil or dry plant material such as leaves to keep the grass from compacting as it settles. Compaction prevents air from entering the pile and slows or prevents the composting process.

- **Dry leaves:** Most leaves decompose faster and more thoroughly if they are shredded before they are added to the pile. If you do not have a shredder, place the leaves in a row on your yard and cut them up with a lawn mower. Rake up the chopped leaves and add them to the compost pile.

- **Manure:** Chicken, cow, and horse manures are excellent nitrogen sources for compost piles. However, never add cat or dog feces in a compost pile because they can carry disease organisms.

- **Sawdust:** Because sawdust can tie up nitrogen in the soil as it decomposes, always compost it before adding it to your garden. Add extra nitrogen to sawdust to speed its breakdown.

- **Other materials:** Sod removed from the lawn, hay, non-noxious weeds, shredded newspaper, and hedge clippings can all be composted. Do not use large twigs because they break down slowly.

Organic materials have varying ratios of carbon (C) to nitrogen (N), which influence how fast the microorganisms can break them down. If the C:N ratio is too high, decomposition will be slow; if the ratio is too low, the pile will lose some nitrogen to the air in the form of ammonia. The ideal C:N ratio for a compost pile is 30:1.

One way of estimating the

Source: allispossible.org.uk (CC BY 2.0)
Kitchen scraps on a compost pile

C:N ratio is by the amount of green and brown materials in the compost pile.

Cut grass, kitchen scraps, and manure are considered green materials and have low C:N ratios.

Sawdust, tree leaves, and straw are brown materials and have high C:N ratios.

Adding an equal amount (by weight) of green and brown materials will give you the right C:N ratio.

Another factor that influences how fast the composting process works is the size of the organic materials. The smaller the item, the faster that the

Source: SuperFantastic (CC BY 2.0)

Steaming compost pile

microorganisms can break it down.

Heat is generated as the microorganisms begin to break down the organic material. Within a few days, the compost pile should reach an internal temperature of 90°F to 160°F. This process will produce rich, soft compost while destroying most weed seeds, insect eggs, and disease organisms.

Tend the pile

To speed up the decomposition, turn the pile weekly in the summer and monthly in the winter. With the proper mixture of ingredients, it should take about 90 to 120 days to prepare good compost.

Below are some common composting problems along with possible causes and solutions.

The compost smells bad: The pile may have either too little air or too much water. Without air, the compost will produce an odor like rotting eggs. Turn the pile to introduce more air.

The compost pile should be moist but not soggy. If you squeeze a handful of the material, it should be damp, but water should not drip out. If the pile is too wet, add dry material and improve the drainage.

The compost is not breaking down, and the center of the pile is dry: The pile does not have enough water, a common problem during the summer. Moisten and turn the pile.

The compost is damp and sweet smelling but does not heat up: The pile may lack nitrogen. Mix in a nitrogen source such as fresh manure or grass clippings.

The compost is damp and warm only in the middle: The pile might not have enough materials or space. Add more material and mix it with the old ingredients into a new, larger pile.

Option: In-ground composting

You can compost materials directly in the ground, preferably where you will plant a garden row next season once they are completely composted.

Source: mjmonty (CC BY 2.0)

A compost turner (center of bin) for aerating the pile

To compost in the ground:
1. Dig up the area—a long row or a raised bed—and remove the soil.
2. Fill the hole with the organic materials, such as shredded newspapers and dry leaves.
3. Cover it up with the original soil.
4. Let this area rest, or compost, for a few months.
5. Turn the soil and use it as a new planting bed.

Source: Scot Nelson (CC BY 2.0)

Diseases

Plants get sick sometimes. But you can minimize the chances of diseases attacking your vegetables by eliminating one or more of these three factors in your garden:

- A susceptible host—a plant or insect where the disease organism can live
- A disease-causing agent, such as a fungus or virus
- The right environmental conditions for that agent, including favorable temperatures, moisture levels, sunlight intensity, or pH levels

If you minimize or remove any of these factors, your garden will have few problems with diseases.

Choose disease-resistant varieties: A plant is resistant to a disease if the pest doesn't eat the plant, cannot live on or in it, or can't multiply on it. Plants that are resistant to a disease will not suffer any damage from it. Resistant varieties are available for many garden vegetable crops.

To determine which varieties are less susceptible to disease, check seed packets and do online research.

Buy disease-free seeds and plants: Don't bring trouble into your garden by introducing serious diseases via seeds and transplants. Get seeds from reputable sources, and inspect the plants before you buy.

Destroy weeds in and near the garden: Some diseases are spread by insects, such as thrips. They can move into your garden from weed patches nearby. Eliminate their breeding grounds by removing weeds.

Source: mealmakeovermoms (CC BY-ND 2.0)

Plants trained to grow upright to avoid contact with soil-borne disease organisms

Plant on raised beds: Elevating the garden allows excess water to move out of the root area and prevents many root diseases and fruit rots.

Space the plants to allow air to circulate: Plant diseases grow best in moist, humid conditions. To encourage the plants to dry quickly after a rain, leave room for them to grow and for air to circulate among them once they're mature.

Train the vegetables to grow upright on cages, fences, or trellises: They keep the fruit from contacting the ground, where many disease organisms live.

Healthy plants do not get diseases as easily as do weak ones.

Water your plants carefully: Protect them by preventing irrigation water from splashing disease agents from the ground onto the plants. Run water between the rows or use a drip irrigation system.

Avoid sprinkling water on the leaves; if you must sprinkle the plants, do so before 10 a.m.

Don't over- or under-fertilize: Plants can suffer from an excess of nutrients as well as a lack. Make your plants less susceptible to disease by making sure they have enough but not too many nutrients.

Clean up debris: After harvest, remove and destroy all the plant materials, where disease organisms may survive to damage next year's crop.

Rotate crops: Because disease organisms often prefer certain types or families of plants, don't plant a variety in a spot where you've planted the same type of vegetable in the past 2 years. Plants of the same family include:

- Broccoli, cabbage, cauliflower, collards, mustard greens, and turnips
- Cucumbers, melons, pumpkins, and squash
- Eggplants, potatoes, and tomatoes

If some of your plants do get a disease, the first step in keeping it from spreading is to remove and destroy all the diseased plants.

Know the causes

Four groups of organisms cause plant diseases: Bacteria, fungi, nematodes, and viruses.

Source: Scot Nelson (CC BY 2.0)

A bacterial disease, black rot of broccoli

If the disease is caused by a bacterium or fungus, the foliage symptoms will normally develop first on the older leaves. If the cause is a virus, the symptoms will appear on the younger leaves first.

Bacteria cells move in the film of water on a leaf surface or in the water surrounding plant roots or soil particles. They are spread most often by splashing water.

These symptoms are indications that a plant has a bacterial disease:

- Leaf lesions (dark spots), sometimes limited by veins
- Ooze streaming from cut tissue
- Soft rot on the fruit with a foul odor

An example of a bacterial disease is black rot in broccoli,

Source: Thomas Isakeit

A fungal disease, downy mildew of cucumber

Brussels sprouts, cabbage, or cauliflower.

Fungi are like tiny plants. Most plant diseases caused by fungi are more severe when temperatures are moderate and water stays on the leaves or fruit for an extended period. Many fungi are spread by wind, equipment such as hoes or spades, and splashing rain.

One sign that a plant problem might be caused by a fungus is the presence of visible fungal structures. They may be seen unaided or with magnification.

Plant diseases caused by fungi include cotton root rot and downy mildew.

Viruses are often spread to healthy plants by insects or a person's hands during normal gardening activities. A plant with a viral disease may have one or more of these symptoms:

- Reduced size
- Mosaic (vein clearing, color break)
- Deformed growth
- Yellows leaves
- Wilting
- Dead spots
- Ring-shaped spots

An example of a disease caused by a virus is yellow leaf mosaic.

Nematodes are small, wormlike animals that live in the soil. They feed on plant roots and cause stunted plants.

The most damaging nematode in home gardens is root knot. It causes galls or knots

Source: Thomas Isakeit

Yellow leaf mosaic, a viral disease, in okra

Galls (tiny round structures) caused by root knot nematodes in potato roots

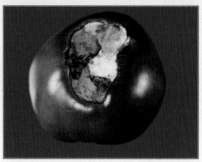

Tomato with blossom end rot, which is caused by a calcium deficiency

on susceptible plants such as beans, cucumbers, squash, tomatoes, and many other vegetables.

Nematodes are best controlled by using a combination of practices. Gardeners can reduce the number of nematodes in the soil by adopting one or more of these practices:

- Plant nematode-resistant varieties.
- Rotate susceptible varieties with plants that are not nematode hosts.
- During the summer after you have removed the plants, till the soil to dry it out.
- Cover the soil with clear plastic and leave it in place for 4 weeks during July.
- Plant Elbon rye during the fall and early winter.

Because nematodes are never eliminated, you will need to take steps each year to control this pest. No chemicals are recommended to control nematodes in home gardens.

Plant disorders

Some vegetable problems are not diseases; they are disorders caused by a lack of nutrients, exposure to pesticides or pollution, or an oversupply of sun, water, or wind.

Examples of plant disorders are blossom end rot of squash and tomatoes, which is caused by a calcium deficiency, and sunscald in peppers and watermelons, which is caused by exposure to too much direct sunlight.

Spot the signs early, and act fast

Plant diseases attack all parts of the plant; they can develop from the time you place the seed in the soil until you eat the vegetable at the table. If you identify disease symptoms quickly, you may be able keep the problem from spreading.

A diseased plant may have one or more of the following symptoms:

- Blotches or other discoloration of the leaves and fruit
- Decayed areas on the fruit or stems
- Deformed leaves
- Stunted leaves, stems, fruit, or the entire plant
- Sudden death of the leaves
- Wilted spots on fruits, leaves, or stems

In some cases, you may need to use a pesticide to control a plant disease. Use these kinds of products carefully and only when needed.

Before using any crop-care product, make sure that the vegetables you need to treat are listed on the label. Read and strictly follow the instructions on the product label.

Note: *Because the pesticides for treating plant diseases change often, any specific product recommendations in this book could be out of date by press time. Check the product label or contact your local county Extension agent for current information.*

To help prevent diseases, space vegetable plants to allow air to circulate between them.

Source: Mark F. Levisay (CC BY 2.0)

Alternaria leaf spot (brown spot)

Source: Aggie Horticulture

Primary vegetables attacked: Broccoli, cabbage, cauliflower, cucumbers, eggplants, greens, melons, squash

Damage: Small, circular spots, each with a yellow halo, on the leaves; as the spot matures, the center becomes sooty black; roots may also become infected when the leaves drop to the ground

Recommendations: Rotate crops; apply an approved fungicide at the first sign of leaf symptoms.

Anthracnose

Source: Scot Nelson (CC BY 2.0)

Primary vegetables attacked: Beans, cucumbers, eggplants, greens, melons, squash, tomatoes

Damage: Leaves covered with small, dry, circular, pale gray to straw-colored spots; severely infected leaves die

Recommendations: Control weeds; make sure that the soil drains well; use approved fungicides.

Ashy stem blight

Source: Thomas Isakeit

Primary vegetables attacked: Beans

Damage: Brown stems with raised black specks

Recommendations: Rotate crops.

Bacterial leaf spot

Source: Scot Nelson (CC BY 2.0)

Primary vegetables attacked: Greens, peppers, radishes, tomatoes

Damage: Small brown spots on the leaves and fruit

Recommendations: Avoid splashing water on the leaves; apply a copper-based fungicide.

Black leg

Source: Thomas Isakeit

Primary vegetables attacked: Broccoli, Brussels sprouts, cabbage, cauliflower, potatoes

Damage: Small spots with ash-gray centers and black dots on the leaves and stems; stem lesions enlarge and extend to the roots; roots develop dry rot; wilted leaves tend to stay attached to the stems instead of falling off

Recommendations: Avoid soils where cabbage or related plants have been grown in the past 4 years; destroy crop debris that has symptoms of the disease.

Black root rot

Source: Thomas Isakeit

Primary vegetables attacked: Carrots

Damage: Roots have small, black-blue areas that expand and girdle the taproot; the roots become constricted at the site of the lesions; black discoloration extends into the root.

Recommendations: Plant resistant varieties on a raised bed in well-drained soil; rotate crops.

Black rot

Source: Scot Nelson (CC BY 2.0)

Primary vegetables attacked: Broccoli, Brussels sprouts, cabbage, cauliflower, greens, sweet potatoes

Damage: Yellow areas along the leaf edges, progressing into the leaf in an inverted-V shape; leaf veins appear to have black to dark gray strands running through them; the damage is first visible on lower leaves

Recommendations: Wait 4 or 5 years before planting vegetables of this family in the same spot; apply bactericides at first sign of leaf infection.

Blossom end rot

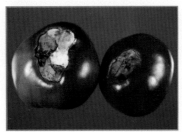

Source: Thomas Isakeit

Primary vegetables attacked: Melons, tomatoes

Damage: The outer end of the fruit is dried and leathery; secondary fungus growth sometimes follows.

Recommendations: Water the plants evenly; apply mulch.

Botrytis rot (gray mold)

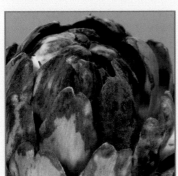

Source: Gerald Holmes, California Polytechnic State University at San Luis Obispo, Bugwood.org

Primary vegetables attacked: Artichokes

Damage: Bracts are brown on the outside with a gray growth inside; the crown is slimy and foul smelling.

Recommendations: Leave plenty of space between plants; do not wet leaves when watering; destroy crop debris after harvest.

Choanephora wet rot

Source: Thomas Isakeit

Primary vegetables attacked: Squash

Damage: Black or gray growth on developing flowers and fruit

Recommendations: Apply a copper-based fungicide.

Crown rot

Source: Aggie Horticulture

Primary vegetables attacked: Asparagus, tomatoes

Damage: Plants are wilted, stunted, and yellowed, and then they dry up and die; reddish-brown decay inside lower stems, crowns, and roots.

Recommendations: Plant tolerant varieties; minimize plant stress; rotate crops.

Damping-off

Source: Thomas Isakeit

Primary vegetables attacked: Carrots, eggplants, greens, melons, peppers, tomatoes

Damage: Seedlings do not emerge, or they wilt and die soon after emergence.

Recommendations: Plant on raised beds to keep the soil from getting too wet.

Downy mildew

Source: Thomas Isakeit

Primary vegetables attacked: Broccoli, Brussels sprouts, cabbage, cauliflower, corn, cucumbers, greens, melons, onions, squash

Damage: Angular yellow spots appear, enlarge, and merge on the tops of the leaves, which then die; gray, fluffy, downy growth in spots on the leaf undersides

Recommendations: Remove or destroy old plant debris; remove weeds; rotate crops, apply preventive fungicide.

Early blight

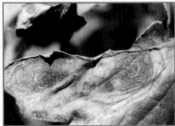

Source: Thomas Isakeit

Primary vegetables attacked: Eggplants, potatoes, tomatoes

Damage: Brown spots that often look like targets

Recommendations: Avoid spraying water on the leaves; apply fungicide.

Fusarium wilt

Source: Thomas Isakeit

Primary vegetables attacked: Cucumbers, melons, okra, peas, potatoes, squash, tomatoes

Damage: Wilted or dead plants; brown streaks near the crown; discolored, honey-brown roots

Recommendations: Plant resistant varieties; wait 4 or 5 years before planting vegetables of the same family in the same spot.

Fusarium yellow

Source: M. E. Bartolo, Bugwood.org

Primary vegetables attacked: Broccoli, Brussels sprouts, cabbage, cauliflower

Damage: Yellowish-green leaves with curved midribs and growth on only one side; wilted, stunted plants

Recommendations: Plant resistant varieties; wait 4 or 5 years before planting vegetables of the same family in the same spot.

Herbicide injury

Source: Scot Nelson (CC BY-SA 2.0)

Primary vegetables attacked: Any

Damage: Twisted, deformed leaves; leaf burn or yellowing; dead or bleached leaf veins; bronzing or speckling of leaves; stunted shoots

Recommendations: None

Iris yellow spot

Source: Thomas Isakeit

Primary vegetables attacked: Onions

Damage: Leaves have diamond-shaped spots with green centers.

Recommendations: None

Iron deficiency

Source: Thomas Isakeit

Primary vegetables attacked: Any

Damage: Yellowing between veins

Recommendations: Acidify the soil or apply iron to the leaves.

Late blight

Source: Thomas Isakeit

Primary vegetables attacked: Eggplants, potatoes, tomatoes

Damage: Spots appear on the leaves, which then wilt, die quickly, and dry out.

Recommendations: Apply fungicide.

Leaf blight

Source: Andrew Pape, Allied Cooperative Pest Pros Division (CC BY-SA 3.0)

Primary vegetables attacked: Carrots

Damage: Indefinite brown to black areas with pale yellow centers; in heavy infestations, leaves shrivel, look as if burned by fire

Recommendations: Apply preventive fungicide where the disease is prevalent.

Leaf mold

Source: Thomas Isakeit

Primary vegetables attacked: Tomatoes

Damage: Velvety gray growth on leaf underside

Recommendations: Apply fungicide; space the plants to allow air to circulate around the leaves.

Leaf spot

Source: Scot Nelson (CC BY 2.0)

Primary vegetables attacked: Carrots, eggplants, herbs, okra, peppers, sweet potatoes

Damage: Circular spots with yellow margins, eventually merging

Recommendations: Rotate crops.

Mosaic

Source: Thomas Isakeit

Primary vegetables attacked: Beans, beets, greens, peppers, potatoes, squash

Damage: Leaves have a greenish-yellow mottle and may be deformed and curved upward; plant is stunted; fruit are deformed.

Recommendations: Keep the garden free of weeds; control insects.

Northern leaf blight

Source: Thomas Isakeit

Primary vegetables attacked: Corn

Damage: Elongated brown spots on the lower leaves

Recommendations: None needed

Phytophthora blight

Source: Thomas Isakeit

Primary vegetables attacked: Eggplants, peppers, tomatoes

Damage: Wilted plants of any age with rotted roots and lower stems; white growth on fruit, which then rots

Recommendations: Rotate crops; plant on raised beds to allow drainage.

Powdery mildew

Source: Thomas Isakeit

Primary vegetables attacked: Artichokes, beans, beets, broccoli, Brussels sprouts, cabbage, carrots, cauliflower, cucumbers, greens, herbs, melons, onions, peas, peppers, radishes, squash, tomatillos, tomatoes

Damage: White, powdery spots appear and enlarge on the leaves; severely infected leaves shrivel and die; plants are yellow and stunted and may die.

Recommendations: Space the plants to allow air to circulate around the leaves; apply protective fungicide.

Purple blotch

Source: Thomas Isakeit

Primary vegetables attacked: Onions

Damage: Leaves have elongated brown spots, often with purplish margins and fuzzy black growth in the centers.

Recommendations: Space the plants to allow air to circulate and the leaves to dry faster; apply fungicide.

Root knot nematodes

Source: Thomas Isakeit

Primary vegetables attacked: Beans, beets, broccoli, Brussels sprouts, cabbage, carrots, cauliflower, greens, okra, onions, potatoes, sweet potatoes, tomatillos, tomatoes

Damage: Irregular swellings and galls on the roots; scab on the tubers; plants wilting in dry periods, stunted; leaves pale green; yields reduced

Recommendations: Rotate crops; plant resistant varieties; solarize the soil.

Root rot

Source: Thomas Isakeit

Primary vegetables attacked: Artichokes, beans

Damage: Wilting or dead plants with brown, rotted roots and lower stems

Recommendations: Rotate crops; plant on raised beds to keep the soil from becoming too wet.

Rust

Source: Thomas Isakeit

Primary vegetables attacked: Asparagus, beans, corn

Damage: Small, velvety spots on the leaves that may be golden, reddish brown, or yellow

Recommendations: Apply fungicide; none needed on corn

Silver leaf

Source: Thomas Isakeit

Primary vegetables attacked: Squash

Damage: White to silvery areas appear and enlarge on the leaves. Silver leaf is not actually a disease but is insect injury caused by whitefly nymphs.

Recommendations: None

Smut

Source: Thomas Isakeit

Primary vegetables attacked: Corn

Damage: Black, deformed growth inside the ears

Recommendations: Rotate crops.

Sooty mold

Source: Thomas Isakeit

Primary vegetables attacked: Cucumbers

Damage: Black growth on the leaves and other plant parts; insects such as aphids and whiteflies also present

Recommendations: Controlling the insects will control the fungi.

Southern blight

Source: Thomas Isakeit

Primary vegetables attacked: Beans, beets, broccoli, Brussels sprouts, cabbage, carrots, cauliflower, melons, okra, peppers, potatoes, tomatoes

Damage: White growth at the base of wilted plants: white growth starts where the fruit touch bare soil; often with fungal structures that look like mustard seeds

Recommendations: Rotate the crop; place mulch under developing fruit; remove affected plants.

Spotted wilt

Source: Thomas Isakeit

Primary vegetables attacked: Tomatoes

Damage: Dead leaves; rings on the fruit

Recommendations: Remove affected plants.

Squash leaf curl

Source: Thomas Isakeit

Primary vegetables attacked: Cucumbers, melons, squash

Damage: Curling, yellowed leaves; stunted growth

Recommendations: None

Sunburn, sunscald

Source: Thomas Isakeit

Primary vegetables attacked: Beans, melons, peppers

Damage: Sunken, bleached area on the fruit caused by direct sun exposure to previously shaded fruit

Recommendations: Prevent leaf loss by controlling bacterial leaf spot, downy mildew, or other problems.

Tobacco mosaic

Source: University of Georgia Plant Pathology Archive, University of Georgia, Bugwood.org (CC BY 3.0 US)

Primary vegetables attacked: Tomatillos, tomatoes

Damage: Wilted, dwarfed plant; yield loss

Recommendations: Destroy the plant.

Turnip mosaic

Source: David B. Langston (CC BY 3.0)

Primary vegetables attacked: Greens

Damage: Mottled, distorted leaves; stunted plant; reduced yield

Recommendations: Control weeds; after harvest, shred the plants.

Verticillium wilt

Source: Aggie Horticulture

Primary vegetables attacked: Artichokes, eggplants, potatoes, tomatoes

Damage: Wilting, then the leaves soon begin to yellow, then turn brown and die

Recommendations: Rotate crops yearly; plant resistant varieties; solarize the soil.

White rust

Source: Scot Nelson (CC BY 2.0)

Primary vegetables attacked: Greens, radishes

Damage: Clusters of white, blister-like raised areas on the leaf underside; faint yellow spots on top

Recommendations: Use resistant cultivars; rotate crops for at least 2 years; remove crop debris.

Yellow leaf curl

Source: Don Ferrin, Louisiana State University Agricultural Center, Bugwood.org (CC BY 3.0 US)

Primary vegetables attacked: Tomatoes

Damage: Stunted plants; curling, yellowed leaves

Recommendations: Remove affected plants.

Yellow leaf mosaic

Source: Thomas Isakeit

Primary vegetables attacked: Okra

Damage: Yellow mosaic pattern on the leaves and pods

Recommendations: Remove affected plants.

Yellow vine

Source: Jim Jasinski, Ohio State University Extension, Bugwood.org (CC BY 3.0 US)

Primary vegetables attacked: Cucumbers, melons, squash, zucchini

Damage: General yellowing of leaves; leaves on the stem ends are turned up; presence of squash bugs

Recommendations: Control the squash bugs before symptoms appear.

Insects and other pests

Garden insects and other visitors can be friends or foes. To keep your garden healthy, know the difference between the good bugs and the bad, recognize that some damage is inevitable, and limit your use of pesticides to avoid killing the allies along with the enemies.

Besides insect pests, other banes of Texas gardens include mites, slugs, and snails. Mammal marauders include deer, gophers, feral hogs, mice, opossums, rabbits, and raccoons. Pets also can pose problems for plants.

The best way to keep pest problems to a minimum is to use a variety of proven tactics that are economical and effective and do the least harm to people, property, and the environment. This approach is called integrated pest management, or IPM. To practice IPM:

- First, do all you can to prevent problems from developing. Keep your plants and soil healthy.

Insect damage

Source: Scot Nelson (CC BY 2.0)

Aphids tended by ants on okra leaf

Source: Scot Nelson (CC BY 2.0)

Insect-feeding injury on kale

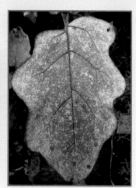

Source: Scot Nelson (CC BY 2.0)

White stippling from spider mite feeding on eggplant

- Next, invest some time and effort into checking your plants regularly for insects and other pests.
- Then determine whether what you find has pest potential. Are they friends or foes?
- If you need to take action, use good information to make good decisions on how to treat the problem.
- Use only proven pest-management tools.

Watch for signs of damage

Insect pests damage garden plants in two primary ways—by chewing holes in the fruit, leaves, roots, or stems; and by sticking their beaks into plant parts and sucking out the juices.

Some insects also spread disease-causing organisms such as bacteria to plants.

- *Chewing insects:* Leave holes and sometimes eat entire plant parts
- *Armyworms:* Eat large holes in the leaves and may eat the fruit
- *Cabbage loopers:* Eat holes in cabbage, collards, and broccoli
- *Corn earworms:* Chew the fruits of tomatoes, peppers, and corn
- *Cutworms:* Cut off plants at or below ground level
- *Grasshoppers:* Eat entire leaves
- *Sucking insects:* Attack fruit, leaves, stems, and vines:
- *Aphids:* Leaves and stems

- *Stink bugs:* Stems and fruit
- *Leafhoppers:* Leaves
- *Squash bugs:* Stems and vines
- *Whiteflies:* Undersides of leaves

In Texas, insects and other pests attack garden plants year-round. Some insects feed on sprouting seed and young seedlings; others chew on growing plants or on mature plants and fruit.

The following symptoms will help you recognize insect problems:

- Stunted plants that do not grow properly
- Deformed or damaged leaves
- Yellow or light-colored plants

- Wilted and droopy plants

If your plants show any of these symptoms, examine each plant for insects. Also check the soil near the plant base, because many insects will drop and hide there when disturbed.

Identify the problem

As with human ailments, the first step in curing the problem is to identify its cause. Then you can determine the right approach to curing it.

Photographs of common garden insects, descriptions of their damage, and control recommendations are at the end of this section.

More information about pest and beneficial insects in vegetable gardens is available on the websites of the Department of Entomology of the Texas A&M AgriLife Extension Service at http://www.texasinsects.org/ and the Vegetable Resources section of the Aggie Horticulture website at http://aggie-horticulture.tamu.edu/vegetable/.

Source: Scot Nelson (CC BY 2.0)

Flea beetle injury to an eggplant leaf

Assassin bug attacking a caterpillar pest

Big-eyed bug eating a whitefly

Common blue damselfly, a garden friend

Don't kill the good guys!

Beneficial organisms pollinate plants, improve the soil through tunneling and decomposition, and help control pests. By allowing beneficials to work for us, we reduce the need for pesticides that could harm the environment.

Beneficial insects include pollinators, decomposers/recyclers, and natural enemies.

Pollinators move pollen from the male parts of plants to the female parts, leading to fertilization and the production of fruits and seeds: Butterflies, honeybees, hover flies, and wasps.

Decomposers/recyclers improve the soil through tunneling and decomposition and include earthworms and termites.

Mealybug destroyer larva

Lady beetle larva

Lady beetle attacking aphids

Praying mantis prey includes crickets, flies, mosquitoes, and moths.

Wheel bug, a predator of garden pests

Natural enemies: Gardens have three main types of natural enemies of insect pests:

- *Predators* hunt and kill other organisms for food. These include assassin bugs, big-eyed bugs, damselflies, ground beetles, lacewings, lady beetles, praying mantises, robber flies, spiders, wasps, and wheel bugs.
- *Parasites and parasitoids* live on or in pests. The difference is that parasites do not kill their hosts, but parasitoids eventually do. Examples are parasitic wasps, parasitic flies, and parasitic nematodes.
- *Pathogens* cause disease in their hosts. A pathogen that is commonly used as a pesticide is *Bacillus thuringiensis (Bt)*, a bacterium that lives in soil, on leaves, and in the gut of caterpillars of some moths and butterflies.

Pupating parasitic wasps on a tomato hornworm

Parasitic wasp laying eggs in a caterpillar

Pollen-dappled bee on a cucumber blossom

Source: bob in swamp (CC BY 2.0)

Wasp shouldering a load of pollen

Source: Leeks 'N' Bounds (CC BY-SA 2.0)

Spider nabbing an intruder

Source: schizoform (CC BY 2.0)

Earthworms improve the soil by aeration and decomposition.

Remember also that if you want to attract butterflies, you'll need to refrain from killing them at the larval stage.

To attract beneficials to the garden, roll out the welcome mat by having the right plants blooming throughout the growing season:

- **Early blooming:** Ajuga, alyssum, columbine, crimson clover, rosemary, and thyme
- **Midseason blooming:** Aster, chamomile, cilantro, lavender, mints, Queen Anne's lace, sedum, and yarrow
- **Late blooming:** Bee balm, dill, fennel, and goldenrod

Take action

You can manage many insects without using pesticides. Below are some of the cultural methods that can help prevent or control insect damage:

- Keep weeds and grass pulled out of the garden.

Source: USDAgov

A spined soldier bug attacking beetle larvae

Source: Gilles San Martin (CC BY-SA 2.0)

Lacewings hunt and kill harmful insects.

Source: Walcoford (CC BY-SA 3.0)

Robber fly with captured fly

Source: OakleyOriginal (CC BY 2.0)

Monarch butterfly larva

Source: ToolManTimTaylor (CC BY 2.0)

Monarch butterfly adult

Mow the area around the garden.

- Plant varieties that grow well in your area.
- Apply the correct amount of fertilizer and water when needed.
- When you have finished harvesting, destroy the old plants by removing them or plowing them under.
- Wash off insects such as aphids and spider mites with a water hose.
- For some species, you could pick the insects or egg masses off the plant by hand and drop them into a pail of soapy water.

However, cultural control takes time and effort. You may need to accept that your plants will have some slight damage. And you may need to use pesticides to control the insects. For best results, treat the insects before large numbers build up in the garden.

Organic insecticides recommended for home vegetable gardens include azadirachtin, *Bacillus thuringiensis* (Bt), garlic juice extract, neem oil, pyrethrins, and spinosad.

Conventional insecticides for home gardens include carbaryl, malathion, and naled.

Before you buy a pesticide, read the label to see if it is recommended to be used on the pest and the plants you want to treat.

Before you apply a pesticide, check the label to see how much you should use. Read all information on the label and follow all the directions.

All insecticides are poisonous, so handle them with care and keep them away from children and pets.

Rogues gallery

Below are photographs, descriptions, control recommendations, and other information about common insect pests of vegetable gardens in Texas.

Remember: When using a pesticide, always follow the cautions, warnings, and directions on the product label.

Source: Bart Drees, Extension Entomology, Texas A&M University

Adult

Aphids

Description: ⅛ inch long, soft bodied, and green, pink, red, brown, or powdery blue; usually found on the leaf underside; may be covered with a fine whitish wax

Primary vegetables attacked: Artichokes, beans, beets, broccoli, Brussels sprouts, cabbage, cauliflower, cucumbers, greens, melons, okra, onions, peppers, potatoes, squash, tomatoes

Damage: Leaves turn yellow; plant may be stunted

Organic control options: Azadirachtin, Bt-based insecticides (Biotrol, Dipel, Thuricide), garlic juice extract, neem oil, pyrethrin, rotenone, sulfur

Source: Jack Kelly Clark, University of California Statewide IPM Program

Larva

Source: aarongunna (CC BY-SA 2.0)

Adult

Artichoke plume moth

Description: **Larvae** are 0.04 to 0.06 inch long, and pale yellow or green; **adults** are buff to brownish buff with a wingspan of ¾ to 1¼ inches

Primary vegetable attacked: Artichokes

Damage: Holes in bracts, new stems, and leaves; the larvae also bore into the stem and buds, and they may bore into the crown underground

Organic control options: Bt-based insecticides (Biotrol, Dipel, Thuricide), sanitation

Source: Kim Hansen (CC BY-SA 3.0 or GFDL)
Adult

Asparagus beetle (spotted)

Description: ¼ inch long, oval, reddish orange with twelve black spots

Primary vegetable attacked: Asparagus

Damage: Spears brown, scarred, bent over into a shepherd's crook; ferns devoured

Organic control options: Remove by hand, Surround (kaolin clay)

Source: Aggie Horticulture
Adult

Banded cucumber beetle

Description: ¼ inch long; yellow-green with three yellow bands

Primary vegetables attacked: Beans, beets, cabbage, corn, cucumbers, greens, okra, onions, peas, squash, sweet potatoes

Damage: Stunted seedlings, holes in leaves, scars on fruit, wilted plant, bore holes in root and stem below soil line

Organic control options: Pyrethrin, rotenone

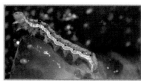

Source: M. Martin Vicente (CC BY 2.0)
Larva

Source: Bennyboymothman
(CC BY 2.0)
Adult

Beet armyworm

Description: 1¼ inches long, green with dark stripes on the side

Primary vegetables attacked: Asparagus, beans, beets, broccoli, cabbage, cauliflower, corn, eggplant, greens, onions, peas, peppers, potatoes, radishes, sweet potatoes, tomatoes

Damage: Holes in the leaves

Organic control options: Azadirachtin, Bt-based insecticides (Biotrol, Dipel, Thuricide) sulphur

Source: John Tann

Larva

Cabbage looper

Description: Up to 1½ inches long; pale green with light stripe down back; doubles up or loops when crawls

Primary vegetables attacked: Beans, beets, broccoli, Brussels sprouts, cabbage, cauliflower, cantaloupes, cucumbers, greens, melons, peas, peppers, potatoes, radishes, squash, sweet potatoes, tomatoes

Damage: Ragged holes in the leaves

Organic control options: Azadirachtin, *Bt*-based insecticides (Biotrol, Dipel, Thuricide), garlic juice extract, pyrethrin

Source: photofarmer (CC BY 2.0)

Larvae

Source: Scott Bauer, USDA ARS

Adult

Colorado potato beetle

Description: **Larvae** are up to ⅜ inch long, soft bodied, and red or light orange; two rows of black dots are on each side; **adults** are ⅜ inch long and have black and yellow stripes

Primary vegetables attacked: Eggplants, potatoes, tomatoes

Damage: Holes in leaves; can defoliate plant

Organic control options: Azadirachtin

Source: Sarah from Statesboro GA, USA (CC BY 2.0)

Larva

Corn earworm (also called tomato fruitworm)

Description: **Larva:** Up to 1¾ inches long; green, brown or pink, light stripes along the sides and on the back; **adult:** Light to dark brown, or light olive green; wingspan about 1½ inches adults are buff to brownish buff with a wingspan of ¾ to 1¼ inches

Primary vegetables attacked: Corn, peppers, tomatoes

Damage: Excrement and feeding damage on leaves, silks, and within the ear

Organic control options: Azadirachtin, *Bt*-based insecticides (Biotrol, Dipel, Thuricide), garlic juice extracts

Source: Jack Kelly Clark, University of California Statewide IPM Program

Adult

Cribrate weevil

Description: ⅓ inch long, brown to black; may appear between June and September

Primary vegetable attacked: Artichokes

Damage: Notched, ragged leaves; heavy infestation may leave only the leaf midrib

Organic control options: Prevent its introduction by using clean transplants, entomopathogenic nematodes *(Steinernema carpocapsae)*

Source: Sam Droege

Larva

Cutworm

Description: Gray to brown with faint, lighter colored stripes, rough skin with variously sized cone-shaped granules

Primary vegetables attacked: Asparagus, beans, cabbage, carrots, corn, eggplants, greens, peas, peppers, potatoes, sweet potatoes, tomatillos, tomatoes

Damage: Stems cut off at the base, larvae feeding inside the fruit and on the leaves, root, and stem

Organic control options: Azadirachtin, *Bt*-based insecticides (Biotrol, Dipel, Thuricide), diatomaceous earth, neem oil, remove by hand, sanitation, spinosad, weed control

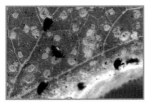

Source: David Cappaert, Michigan State University, Bugwood.org

Adults

Eggplant flea beetle

Description: 1/16 inch long, light markings, bronze-black, blue, or green; jumps quickly

Primary vegetable attacked: Eggplant

Damage: Holes in the leaves

Organic control options: Diatomaceous earth, neem oil, spinosad

Source: Keith Weller

Larva

Source: ©entomart

Adult

European corn borer

Description: **Larvae** are pinkish tan; **adults** are tan, ½ inch long, and hold their wings in a delta shape at rest

Primary vegetable attacked: Corn

Damage: Small pinholes and straw-like excrement on the leaves, small holes in the stalk

Organic control options: Azadirachtin, *Bt*-based insecticides (Biotrol, Dipel, Thuricide), garlic juice extract

---

Source: Bart Drees, Extension Entomology, Texas A&M University

Mature larva

Source: Andy Reago & Chrissy McClarren (CC BY 2.0)

Adult

Fall armyworm

Description: **Young larvae** have a light-colored body and a black head; **mature larvae** are 1⅓ inches long with three yellowish white lines down the back; **adults** are ¾ inch long and 1½ inches wide and have gray wings and irregular white spots

Primary vegetable attacked: Corn

Damage: Ragged-edged holes on leaves, tassels, ears; sawdust-like excrement on leaves; chewed kernels

Organic control options: Azadirachtin, *Bt*-based insecticides (Biotrol, Dipel, Thuricide), garlic juice extract, kaolin clay, spinosad

---

Source: bob in swamp (CC BY 2.0)

Adults

Flea beetle

Description: ¹⁄₁₆ inch long; black, black-bronze, blue, brown-black with light markings, green, or metallic bronze; jumps quickly

Primary vegetables attacked: Beans, beets, cabbage, corn, eggplants, greens, melons, peas, peppers, potatoes, radishes, sweet potatoes, tomatoes

Damage: Holes in leaves, holes and tunnels in tubers, brown or gray lines on corn leaves

Organic control options: Azadirachtin, Bt-based insecticides (Biotrol, Dipel, Thuricide), crop rotation, garlic juice extract, kaolin clay, plant resistant varieties, sulfur

Source: Babbage (CC BY-SA 4.0)

Adult

Grasshoppers

Description: Large body, long back legs for jumping, conspicuous eyes, usually brown, gray, green, or yellowish

Primary vegetables attacked: Broccoli, Brussels sprouts, cabbage, cauliflower, greens, radishes

Damage: Holes in the leaves

Organic control options: Azadirachtin, garlic juice extracts, kaolin clay, pyrethrin

Source: Ton Rulkens (CC BY-SA 2.0)

Adult

Harlequin bug

Description: Black and yellow; shield shaped; up to ⅜ inch long

Primary vegetables attacked: Broccoli, Brussels sprouts, cabbage, cauliflower, greens, radishes

Damage: Plant wilted, leaves turn brown

Organic control options: Azadirachtin, garlic juice extract, pyrethrin

Source: cbede (CC BY 2.0)

Adult

Hornworm

Description: Green, 3 inches long, with a horn on one end and stripes on the side

Primary vegetable attacked: Tomatoes

Damage: Holes in the leaves and fruit

Organic control options: Azadirachtin, *Bt*-based insecticides (Biotrol, Dipel, Thuricide)

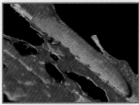

Source: Harald Süpfle (CC BY-SA 3.0)
Larva

Source: Kleiner_Kohlweissling_
Pieris_rapae_Profil.jpg (CC BY-SA 2.5)
Adult

Imported cabbage worm

Description: Velvety green, up to 1¼ inches long, with three faint gold stripes on the back

Primary vegetables attacked: Broccoli, Brussels sprouts, cabbage, cauliflower, greens

Damage: Large, irregular holes in leaves, boreholes in head

Organic control options: Azadirachtin, *Bt*-based insecticides (Biotrol, Dipel, Thuricide), garlic juice extract, pyrethrin, spinosad

Source: platycryptus (CC BY 2.0)
Adult

Leafhopper

Description: Green, up to ⅛ inch long, wedge shaped; crawls sideways when disturbed

Primary vegetables attacked: Beans, eggplants, greens, potatoes

Damage: Leaves curl upward and turn yellow to brown

Organic control options: Kaolin clay

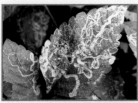

Source: Scot Nelson (CC BY 2.0)
Damage

Source: Jerry A. Payne
(CC BY 3.0)
Larvae

Leafminer

Description: Small, yellowish larvae inside the leaves

Primary vegetables attacked: Beans, cantaloupes, cucumbers, eggplants, greens, melons, potatoes, peas, squash, tomatoes

Damage: Tunnels or trails on the leaves

Organic control options: Azadirachtin, biological controls (Dacsure, Disureigsure), diatomaceous earth, neem oil, remove infected leaves, spinosad

Source: Franco Fzolini (CC BY 2.5)
Adult

Source: ljguitar (CC BY 2.0)
...rolled up

Pill bugs

Description: ⅜ to ¾ inch long when full grown; dark gray to black; they roll up into a ball when disturbed; they are not insects but crustaceans; found under plant debris and other objects lying on damp ground

Primary vegetables attacked: Melons, squashes, and other plants with fruits that touch the ground

Damage: Mainly nuisance pests; occasionally damage roots, seedlings, foliage, and fruit that contact the soil

Organic control options: Destroy breeding and hiding sites by eliminating unnecessary boards, stones, and piles of leaves or mulch; reduce moisture by allowing the soil to dry out between waterings; train vines on trellises; raise melons above the soil.

Source: Susan Wineriter, USDA Agricultural Research Service, Bugwood.org (CC BY 3.0 US)
Adult

Psyllid

Description: ¹⁄₁₀ inch long, greenish to black, with a white fringe band around the first abdomen and clear wings held over the back when at rest

Primary vegetable attacked: Tomatoes

Damage: First the midribs and edges of the top leaves and then the entire top of plant turn yellow or purple; leaves stay small and narrow; fruit abnormal, immature

Organic control options: Azadirachtin, insecticidal soap, sulfur

Source: Stefan Jaronski, USDA ARS
Larvae

Adult
Source: berniedup
(CC BY-SA 2.0)

Root maggot

Description: Yellowish white, ¼ to ⅓ inch long, legless

Primary vegetables attacked: Broccoli, Brussels sprouts, cabbage, carrots, cauliflower, onions, radishes, turnips

Damage: Scars, discolored, debris-filled tunnels in the roots

Organic control options: Beneficial insects, crop rotation, and sanitation

Adult Source: Tobyotter (CC BY 2.0)

Source: goldberg (CC BY 2.0)
Damage

Slugs

Description: ¼ to 4 inches long, fleshy, soft, slimy, legless, and gray, black, rusty orange, or whitish yellow

Primary vegetables attacked: All

Damage: Irregular holes with smooth edges in leaves, flowers, and fruit

Organic control options: Barriers, diatomaceous earth, handpicking, slug traps, eliminating hiding places and leaf litter

Source: Marcus T Ward (CC BY-ND 2.0)
Adult

Source: Forban300 (CC BY 2.0)
Damage

Snails

Description: Fleshy, soft, slimy, legless body that can be brown, gray, tan, or white, and has a ¼- to 3-inch shell that can be white, brown, or black and is often striped or mottled

Primary vegetables attacked: All

Damage: Irregular holes with smooth edges in leaves, flowers, and fruit

Organic control options: Barriers, handpicking, slug traps, eliminating hiding places and leaf litter

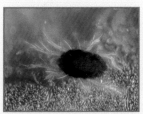

Source: Gilles San Martin from Namur, Belgium (CC BY-SA 2.0)
Adult

Spider mites

Description: Barely visible, spiderlike; may form tiny webs

Primary vegetables attacked: Artichokes, beans, eggplants, melons

Damage: Light dots on the leaves, which lose color and drop off

Organic control options: Beneficial insects (lady beetle), diatomaceous earth, insecticidal soap, neem oil, spinosad, strong blast of water

Source: Pollinator at en.wikipedia (GFDL, CC-BY-SA-3.0, or CC BY 2.5)

Adult

Spotted cucumber beetle

Description: ¼ inch long, yellow-green with 12 black spots

Primary vegetables attacked: Cucumbers, melons, squash

Damage: Stunted seedlings, holes in leaves, scars on fruit, wilted plant

Organic control options: Azadirachtin, pyrethrin

Source: Noel Feans (CC BY 2.0)

Adult

Source: Simply Vicki (CC BY 2.0)

Damage

Squash bug

Description: Up to 1 inch long; gray-brown, reddish brown when small; flat back

Primary vegetables attacked: Cucumbers, pumpkins, squash

Damage: Speckles on leaves, which then turn yellow to brown, and brittle; wilted plant

Organic control options: Azadirachtin

Source: Jim Jasinski, Ohio State University Extension, Bugwood.org (CC BY 3.0 US)

Larva and damage

Source: xinem (CC BY 2.0)

Adult

Squash vine borer

Description: About 1 inch long; usually found inside the stem near the ground

Primary vegetable attacked: Squash

Damage: Vines wilt and die.

Organic control options: Azadirachtin, *Bt*-based insecticides (Biotrol, Dipel, Thuricide) for prevention, as the larvae can't be controlled once they are inside the stem

Source: Extension Entomology, Texas A&M University

Adult

Stink bug

Description: Usually about ½ inch long; brown, green, or black; shield shaped; discharges a foul odor

Primary vegetables attacked: Beans, corn, eggplants, okra, peas, peppers, squash, tomatoes

Damage: Curled pods, wart-like growths on pods

Organic control options: Azadirachtin, insecticidal soap, pyrethrin

Source: Graham Wise (CC BY 2.0)

Adult

Sweet potato weevil

Description: **Adult** is ¼ inch long and has a metallic blue abdomen, black head, and orange to reddish brown antennae, thorax, and legs; the snout projects forward; **larva** is white, C-shaped with a pale brown head, legless and up to ⅓ inch long

Primary vegetable attacked: Sweet potatoes

Damage: Yellowed vines, holes and tunnels in tubers

Organic control options: Azadirachtin, garlic juice extract

Source: Daiju Azuma (CC BY-SA 2.5)

Adult

Thrips

Description: **Adults** are 0.05 inch long, yellowish, with hair-fringed wings usually held across the back; **immatures** look like the adults but are wingless and pale yellow to light brown

Primary vegetables attacked: Onions, lettuce

Damage: Silvery, whitish spots and strips on the leaves, reduced bulb size, scars on bulb

Organic control options: Azadirachtin, spinosad, kaolin clay

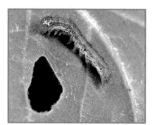

Source: Clemson University - USDA Cooperative Extension Slide Series, Bugwood.org (CC BY 3.0 US)

Larva

Tobacco budworm

Description: Yellowish or yellowish green with a yellowish brown head; later stages are greenish with whitish bands and a brown head capsule; body has many black, thorn-like microspines, giving the body a rough feel

Primary vegetable attacked: Tomatillos

Damage: Holes in young leaves

Organic control options: Azadirachtin, *Bt*-based insecticides (Biotrol, Dipel, Thuricide) sulfur dust

Source: Frank Peairs, Colorado State University, Bugwood.org (CC BY 3.0 US)

Larva

Webworm

Description: 1 inch long, green and yellow with black stripes and spots on the back

Primary vegetable attacked: Beets

Damage: Holes in young leaves

Organic control options: Azadirachtin, *Bt*-based insecticides (Biotrol, Dipel, Thuricide), sulfur dust

Source: gbohne from Berlin, Germany

Adult

Source: Scot Nelson (CC BY 2.0)

Nymphs and damage

Whitefly

Description: **Adults** are tiny with white wings; **nymphs** are oval, whitish, and scale-like and do not move

Primary vegetables attacked: Tomatillos, tomatoes

Damage: Leaves yellow and curl, then blacken and become shiny; fruit ripens unevenly

Organic control options: Azadirachtin, insecticidal soaps, pyrethrin

Larvae

Wireworm

Description: Up to 1½ inches long, smooth, soft bodied, yellow to white; curls up when touched

Primary vegetables attacked: Carrots, corn, potatoes

Damage: Small pinholes and straw-like excrement on the leaves, small holes in the stalk

Organic control options: Azadirachtin, *Bt*-based insecticides (Biotrol, Dipel, Thuricide), removal by hand, sanitation, weed control

Mammals and birds

Below is information on non-insect garden trespassers and options for handling them.

Armadillo

Description: Grayish, armor-plated, 2½ feet long (nose to tip of tail), 8 to 17 pounds

Primary vegetable attacked: Corn

Damage: Burrowing damage

Organic control options: 5- to 6-foot fence or a two-wire electric fence; trapping; repellents may help temporarily

Sparrow downing a grasshopper

Birds

Prime suspects: Baltimore orioles, blackbirds, cedar waxwings, crows, grackles, house finches, mockingbirds, robins, sparrows, starlings

Primary vegetables attacked: Cabbage, corn, eggplants, greens, peas, peppers, tomatoes

Damage: Seeds or seedlings missing; ragged leaves; fruit consumed or left with ragged holes pecked in it

Mitigating factors: Many eat insect pests.

Organic control options: Row covers for newly planted crops; paper bags placed on corn ears after the silks are brown; scare devices such as fluttering objects or reflective tape may help temporarily

Feeding injury to tomatoes

Source: mcmzorgan08 (CC BY-SA 2.0)

Cats

Damage: Plants dug up, crushed; feces left in garden

Mitigating factors They eat rodents.

Organic control options: Water spray when caught in the act; chicken wire or netting laid on or over beds; odor repellents may help temporarily

Source: vladeb (CC BY-ND 2.0)
White-tailed deer

Deer

Primary vegetables attacked: Almost any garden vegetable, but especially beans, broccoli, cabbage, carrots, corn, greens, peas, pumpkins, and tomatoes

Damage: Leaves, shoots, and stems eaten, with ragged edges left on stems and branches; trampled plants

Organic control options: Tall (up to 8-foot) wire mesh fence; three- to five-wire electric fence; alternating repellents with different odors may help temporarily

Source: boboroshi (CC BY 2.0)
Damage on corn

Source: *~Dawn~* (CC BY 2.0)
Mule deer

Source: OakleyOriginals (CC BY 2.0)

Dogs

Damage: Trampled plants; holes dug, urine and feces left in garden

Mitigating factors: They scare away rodents and other mammal pests.

Organic control options: Fencing; training; odor repellents may help temporarily

Source: Texas A&M AgriLife Extension Service

Feral hog

Description: At maturity, 36 inches tall at shoulder; 100 to over 400 pounds, 5 to 6 feet long (snout to tip of tail); coarse, bristly coat that can be solid, spotted, or mottled black, red-brown, dark brown, or white

Primary vegetables attacked: All, corn, greens, melons, nuts, berries, potatoes, roots, crops, plants, seeds, seedlings, mature crops, fruit

Damage: Plants trampled, eaten; rooting damage; holes dug up to 5 feet wide and 2 to 3 feet deep

Organic control options: Snaring, trapping; for more information, see http://feralhogs.tamu.edu/

Source: sfbaywalk (CC BY 2.0)

Gopher

Description: 6 to 13 inches long, up to 1 pound, light brown to deep chocolate fur, prominent yellow incisor teeth, stout front legs with strong, curved claws

Primary vegetable attacked: Roots, tops, and seeds of plants; potatoes

Damage: Dead plants, feeding on vegetables

Mitigating factors: They till and aerate the soil.

Organic control options: Trapping; hardware cloth or ¾-inch mesh poultry wire buried at least 2 feet deep and an extra 6 inches of cloth or wire bent at a 90-degree angle away from the plants

Source: zenera (CC BY-SA 2.0)

Mole and molehills

Source: Pink Sherbet Photography (CC BY 2.0)

Mole

Description: Up to 7 inches long; 4 ounces; grayish brown fur; furless, pointed snouts; small eyes; no external ears; forelegs webbed to the base of the claws

Mitigating factors: Their diet consists mostly of grubs, beetles, and insect larvae); they till and aerate the soils

Damage: Uprooted plants

Organic control options: Castor beans planted around the garden; flushing out moles with water and then trapping them; small mesh or tightly woven hardware cloth fencing slightly above the soil surface and buried 18 to 24 inches below ground; trapping

Opossum

Source: Dawn Huczek (CC BY 2.0)
Adult

Source: /\ \/\/ /\ (CC BY-SA 2.0)
Damage on a watermelon

Description: Adults—black to gray fur, 4 to 15 pounds, 24 to 34 inches long, pointed face, ratlike tail, and round, hairless ears

Primary vegetable attacked: Many kinds of fruits, berries, and greens

Damage: Missing or marred garden produce

Mitigating factors: Their primary food is animal matter such as insects, small rodents, and snails.

Organic control options: 5- to 6-foot fence or a two-wire electric fence; trapping and relocating (best to notify the Texas Parks and Wildlife Department); repellents may help temporarily

Rabbits

Source: sonstroem (CC BY 2.0)
Cottontail

Source: goingslo (CC BY 2.0)
Jackrabbit

Description: **Cottontails**—14 to 17 inches long, 2 to 4 pounds, brown to reddish brown fur, large ears, cottony white tail; **jackrabbits**—17 to 21 inches long, 4 to 8 pounds; grayish brown fur, large, black-tipped ears; black streak on top of the tail

Primary vegetable attacked: Beans, beets, broccoli, carrots, greens, peas

Mitigating factor: Inherent cuteness

Damage: Leaves, shoots, and flowers eaten; plants chewed to the ground; smooth, 45-degree angle cuts left on stems and branches

Organic control options: Around the garden, a 3-foot-high, ¾-inch mesh fence, with 1 foot buried in the ground and 2 feet above ground; remove weedy areas and piles of brush, lumber, and rocks; around individual plants, wire mesh cylinders; repellents may provide some short-term control; trapping (to trap and relocate rabbits, it's best to notify the Texas Parks and Wildlife Department)

Source: Richard Arthur Norton (1958) (CC BY 2.5)
Crabgrass

Source: blumenbiene (CC BY 2.0)
Nutsedge

Source: David~O (CC BY 2.0)
Henbit

Source: pellaea (CC BY 2.0)
Common purslane

Weeds

Weeds compete with plants for water, nutrients, and light and can harbor pests. Weedy gardens produce less than those that are weed free.

Preventive measures: When preparing seedbeds, pull up and destroy all the weeds.

Mulch, mulch, mulch: It can save you hours of weeding. Mulch can be organic (such as leaves) or inorganic (plastic). Organic mulch should be several inches thick.

Attack early: Control weeds in the first few weeks after planting. Pull them up by hand or with a hoe, fork, or spade. Hand-pull weeds growing close to the vegetables to avoid injuring their roots. The best time to weed is when the soil is moist but not wet.

Solarize the soil: Solarizing uses the sun to heat the soil to temperatures that kill weeds as well as insects and bacteria.

At least 6 weeks before planting, clear out all plants and debris, and water the soil deeply until it is very wet.

Cover the area with clear plastic (such as 1 to 4 mil painters plastic). Don't use white or black plastic because they don't let enough heat get to the soil.

Bury the plastic edges to keep in the heat; leave the plastic there for 4 weeks in July, or longer at other times of the year.

Chemical control: Herbicides can control weeds under some conditions; none works on all weeds or can be used on all crops. Many herbicides will kill the crops along with the weeds.

If you use chemicals, follow the directions on the label. Never use an herbicide on a vegetable plant that is not specifically listed on the label.

Harvest, handling, and storage

To reap the best rewards of all your hard work in the garden, harvest your vegetables at their peak maturity, handle them properly, and store them under optimum conditions.

Except for ripening, storage does not improve a vegetable's quality—it must be of good quality at harvest. To determine when your vegetables should reach peak quality, keep a record of what you planted and when.

Guidelines on when and how to harvest specific types of vegetables are included in the "Individual Vegetable Recommendations" section.

Vegetables continue their life processes even after harvest. If the vegetables are mature when you pick them, slow

Source: penelope waits (CC BY 2.0)

Wash snow peas immediately after harvest.

down these life processes by chilling them. If they are immature, such as tomatoes when they're green, store them at room temperature to enhance the ripening process.

Some vegetables need to be washed in cold running water immediately after harvest to remove any contaminants and help lower their temperature. These include beets, cauliflower, celery, greens, lettuce, peas, okra, and radishes.

You should wait to wash other vegetables—such as asparagus, potatoes, and sweet potatoes—until just before using them.

Avoid bruising and cutting vegetables during handling. Toss or recycle any vegetable materials with signs of decay or rot to prevent them from affecting the good produce.

Storage

Three factors that affect produce quality after harvest are temperature, moisture, and ventilation.

- **Temperature:** For produce such as peas and sweet corn, it is critical that you interrupt the conversion of sugar to starch at harvest. To minimize this conversion, cool them immediately. If possible, harvest them early in the morning or just before you intend to use them.

- **Moisture:** The proper humidity level for storage varies. Leafy vegetables require a humidity of about 95 percent; onions can be stored at 65 to 70 percent relative humidity.

- **Ventilation:** To minimize wilting and tissue breakdown, make sure that air can circulate properly.

After harvest is complete, clean up the garden to remove harborage for diseases and insect pests.

Individual Vegetable Recommendations

Source: Bill Watson

Artichokes

Best varieties for Texas

- **Emerald:** Grown from seeds; reaches maturity about 2 weeks earlier than does Imperial Star; appears to need little, if any, chilling temperatures while growing
- **Grand Beurre:** Grown from seeds
- **Green Globe:** Standard variety
- **Harmony**
- **Imperial Star:** Less vigorous than Green Globe
- **Madrigal**
- **Purple Sicilian:** Purple globe; grown from seeds; fairly tolerant of heat and cold
- **Talpiot:** Grown from seeds

Choose the site

Artichokes produce best in deep, fertile, well-drained soil; however, they will grow in a wide range of soils. The plant needs relatively deep soils to allow the roots to develop. Avoid sandy soils with excessive drainage.

Although artichokes are moderately salt tolerant, they will yield less if grown in soil with a high salt content.

Prep the soil

Artichokes grow well if they are fertilized regularly. Have your soil tested and fertilize according to the test results and recommendations. If a soil test is not done, follow these general recommendations:

- Before planting, mix into the soil 100 to 140 pounds of composted manure per 100 square feet.
- Then, also for every 100 square feet, work into the soil about ¼ pound of phosphorus, ¼ pound of potassium, and ⅒ pound of nitrogen.

Artichoke in bloom

Plant

It can take up to 60 days before artichokes grow big enough to be planted outside. In Central and East Texas, transplant artichokes in mid-October, which means that you must start the seeds in mid-August. Gardeners in North and West Texas should start the seeds a few weeks earlier.

In South Texas, frost or freeze is usually not an issue, so you can plant in October through December.

The seeds can easily be started in a greenhouse, in a shady spot outside in late summer, or indoors under a grow light. Plant the seeds ¼ inch deep in potting mix when the temperature doesn't exceed 85°F. Water them regularly and shade them from the hot afternoon sun.

Transplant the seedlings 2½ to 3 feet apart in rows 3 to 4 feet apart. Transplants grow slowly in the fall and winter (October through January), but grow fast in early spring.

Fertilize

Apply ⅓ pound of nitrogen per 100 square feet 6 to 8 weeks after planting. Apply a liquid fertilizer containing calcium and zinc to the leaves every 2 weeks during active growth in early spring.

Water

Artichokes have deep roots and require adequate moisture when growing and producing.

Moisture stress may cause black tip, which mars the appearance but does not affect the edible part of the bud. Black tip is most common when the weather is sunny, warm, and windy.

A hot, dry climate causes artichoke buds to open quickly

Source: Greencolander (CC BY 2.0)

Artichoke transplants grow slowly in fall and winter but fast in early spring.

and become tough. Water the artichokes in the summer to reduce temperatures in the crop canopy and prevent bud opening.

Care

Do not expose artichokes to temperatures below 25°F. If frost is forecast, cover the plants with a 6-inch layer of straw mulch or leaves, a bucket or frost blanket, or some other form of frost protection.

Add mulch to reduce weeds and conserve soil moisture. Remove the weeds when the artichokes are small, when they are most susceptible to weed competition. Large, fully developed artichoke plants compete well with weeds.

Diseases

Common diseases of artichokes in Texas are bacterial crown rot, black tip, botrytis rot, damping-off, powdery mildew, root rot, and Verticillium wilt.

To reduce the chance of diseases, leave plenty of space between the plants for air circulation and do not let the soil become too wet.

For more information, descriptions, control recommendations, and photos of common vegetable diseases, see the "Diseases" section starting on page 40. Before using a pesticide, read the label and always follow cautions, warnings, and directions.

Insects

The most common insect pests are aphids, artichoke plume moths, cribrate weevils, and spider mites.

Photographs, descriptions, and control recommendations for common vegetable insect pests are in the "Insects and other pests" section starting on page 61.

Harvest

A healthy plant should produce six to nine buds per plant.

Harvest after early fall frosts or in very early spring before the new growth starts. The main harvest usually occurs in April and May.

Select buds for their size, compactness, and age. Harvest them by cutting the stem 2 to 3 inches below the base of the bud.

Source: magpie-moon (CC BY 2.0)

Choose artichokes for the size and compactness of their buds.

Store

Refrigerate unwashed artichokes in a plastic bag for up to 4 days.

Cleanup

To allow new stems to grow, remove the old stems as soon as you have harvested all the buds. Cut the plant back to the soil level. This will put the plant crown into a dormant stage during the summer.

The plant will send out shoots in the fall. You may leave them in place to produce another year or dig out the new shoots and replant them in a new location in the garden.

Leave only the most vigorous shoot on the old plant for production next spring.

Asparagus

Best varieties for Texas

- Jersey Giant
- Jersey Knight
- Jersey Supreme
- Purple Passion

Choose the site

Because asparagus remains in the same place several years, it is important to select the right spot and prepare the seedbed well. Asparagus does best in full sunlight and deep, well-drained, sandy, or light-textured soils.

The plants also make a good border around the edge of a garden or along a fence.

Prep the soil

Asparagus does not grow well in soil with a pH of below 6.0. Test the soil and add lime, if needed, to adjust the pH to at least 6.5 to possibly 7.5.

Before planting, make sure that the soil is free of trash, soil insects, and perennial weeds such as johnsongrass or ber-

mudagrass. Avoid sites where yellow nutsedge grows, as it indicates poor drainage, which is unsuitable for asparagus production.

Till the asparagus beds and mark rows 5 feet apart. Dig a furrow 4 inches wide and 4 to 12 inches deep.

Plant

Asparagus is grown from 1- or 2-year-old crowns planted in January or February, or as soon as the ground can be worked. You may also grow crowns from seeds planted in flats or peat cups.

It takes at least a year to grow a good crown. To shorten the period from planting to harvest, buy and plant healthy, vigorous, 1- or 2-year-old crowns from a garden center or online.

Separate the crowns by size, and plant those of similar size together for best uniformity in spear size at harvest.

Spread super phosphate fertilizer (0-46-0) as a band in the

furrow at a rate of 2 pounds per 1,000 square feet or ¾ ounce per 20-foot row.

Place the crowns 12 to 14 inches apart in the furrow. If you plant them too close, the spears will be small. If you plant them more than 14 inches apart, the spears will be large but the overall yield at harvest will be smaller.

In loose soils, plant the crowns 6 to 12 inches deep; in heavier soils, plant them 4 to 6 inches deep.

Cover the furrow with 1 inch of compost topped by 2 to 3 inches of soil. Firm the soil around the roots.

Source: Sigfrid Lundberg (CC BY-SA 2.0)

Asparagus crowns at planting

Over the season, gradually fill the furrows with soil as the shoots grow. This covers small weeds, which will die from lack of light. By the end of the first season, the furrow should reach its normal level.

Or, you could plant the crowns at the suggested depth and immediately fill in the furrow with soil to its original level. Using this method, you do not need to gradually cover the crowns with soil, as long as the soil does not become compacted over the newly planted crowns.

It takes 2 to 3 years from the time the crown is planted until the bed is in full production. When conditions are favorable, buds will grow from the crown and develop into edible spears.

If not harvested, the spears will develop into fernlike stalks. From these stalks, the mature plant manufactures food and stores it in the underground crown. This reserve supplies the energy necessary to produce spears the following year.

Fertilize

Before planting a new asparagus bed, spread and spade in ¼ pound of nitrogen, phosphate, and potassium per

20 feet of row or as directed by a soil test report.

For established beds, scatter 2 pounds of 10-20-10 fertilizer (or its equivalent) per 20 feet of row before growth begins in the spring, late January, or early February in most areas of Texas. Till the soil when you apply the fertilizer.

After the last harvest, apply an additional 1 to 2 pounds per 20 feet of row. If available, use a nitrogen fertilizer such as 21-0-0. Always water the fertilizer into the soil.

Water

Asparagus plants need frequent, deep watering. Water the beds thoroughly, and allow the top 1 inch of soil to dry before watering again. The time varies from 3 to 5 days, depending on soil type and temperature. In sandy soils, asparagus roots can reach 10 feet deep if adequate soil moisture is available.

Care

Asparagus competes poorly with weeds. For asparagus to grow vigorously, control weeds in the first 1 to 2 years of its establishment.

To suppress weeds, spread

Source: sacratomato_hr (CC BY-SA 2.0)
Mature asparagus plant

a 4- to 6-inch-thick layer of organic mulch, such as hay, straw, compost, wood chips, or grass clippings over the bed.

Although you need to control weeds, do not injure the crowns. If you planted the crowns deep, you could cultivate the bed with garden tools or a tiller without damaging the crowns.

Asparagus beds require little care after the first 2 years. Keep the weeds pulled or hoed from the beds. To avoid damaging the spears, remove the weeds early before the spears emerge.

If you use the herbicide Roundup (glyphosate) to control weeds, spray them before the asparagus begins growing in early spring or after the last harvest before ferns develop. To avoid injuring the crown, make sure that no spears are present when applying Roundup.

To grow white asparagus, cover the row with black plastic supported by wire hoops. Open the covering on one side for harvest, and then place it into position again immediately afterward.

Remove the plastic tunnel structure after the harvest season.

Diseases

Common diseases of asparagus in Texas are crown rot, gray mold, leaf spot, purple spot, and rust.

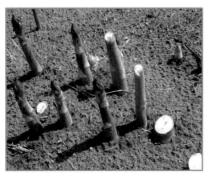

allispossible.org.uk (CC BY 2.0)
Asparagus during harvest

For more information, descriptions, control recommendations, and photos of common vegetable diseases, see the "Diseases" section starting on page 40. Before using a pesticide, read the label and always follow cautions, warnings, and directions.

Insects

The most common insect pests are asparagus beetles, beet armyworms, cutworms, grasshoppers, and thrips.

Photographs, descriptions, and control recommendations for common vegetable insect pests are in the "Insects and other pests" section starting on page 61.

Harvest

Do not harvest during the first 2 years after planting. This waiting period enables the underground crown to grow and store enough reserves for a strong harvest for many years to come.

In established beds, harvest asparagus spears for about 8 weeks, depending on the area. Harvest the spears when they are 4 to 10 inches long. The stalks should be fresh and firm with compact, closed tips; angular or flat stalks are apt to be woody.

To keep the spears from becoming stringy, harvest at least every other day. They become stringy when they get too mature or when the soil is poor. Spears with loose or opened heads are too mature.

To harvest, snap off the spears at ground level by hand. Never snap asparagus spears above the ground or allow a stub to remain.

Also, do not use a knife to cut the spears because the knife may spread diseases from crown to crown.

Stop harvesting when the spears become less than ⅜ inch in diameter or when the spear heads open up with rising temperatures.

To harvest white asparagus, use a knife to cut the spears at the desired height when the asparagus head barely emerges through the mulch mound.

Store

After harvest, asparagus loses quality very rapidly––the sugar content declines and the spears become stringy. Use the spears with compact heads; those with loose heads are fibrous and do not keep well.

Store asparagus up to 3 weeks in plastic bags in the refrigerator. For longer storage, blanch the spears for 3 to 5 minutes, and then package and freeze them.

Cleanup

At the end of the harvest season, control weeds by raking lightly or mulching. Apply fertilizer and till lightly 1 to 2 inches deep to kill the weeds. Cover the bed with a 3-inch layer of compost, clean straw, or other mulch material.

Water the asparagus thoroughly and allow it to grow the rest of the year to ensure a good harvest the next year.

After the first hard frost or freeze of fall, cut off the fern tops at ground level and burn or compost them to eliminate sources of insect eggs or diseases.

In late fall, spread a 3-inch layer of organic matter such as manure, rotted sawdust, or compost over the beds. Till or spade it to a depth of 10 to 12 inches, and turn the soil to cover all organic matter.

Beans

Best varieties for Texas

- **Lima beans:** Florida Butter, Florida Speckled, Fordhook, Henderson Bush, Jackson Wonder
- **Pinto beans:** Dwarf Horticultural, Luna, UI-114
- **Snap beans:** Blue Lake, Derby, Early Contender, Goldencrop Wax, Greencrop, Kentucky Wonder, Tendercrop, Tendergreen, Topcrop

Choose the site

Although beans do well in most Texas soils, they grow best in well-drained soil and with plenty of sunlight.

Prep the soil

Before planting beans, remove all weeds and trash from the planting area.

Work the garden soil when it is dry enough to not stick to the garden tools. Till 8 to 10 inches deep and rake it several times to break up the large clods.

Plant

In the spring, plant the beans after all danger of frost has passed. In the fall, plant them 10 to 12 weeks before the first expected frost.

If possible, use fungicide-treated seeds to protect the seedlings from diseases until they are up and growing. Do not eat treated seeds.

Bush beans: Plant the seeds about 1 inch deep and 1 to 2 inches apart in the row. The rows should be 2½ to 3 feet apart.

After the beans have sprouted, thin them to 3 to 4 inches apart.

Pole beans: Plant the seeds in rows 3 to 4 feet apart. Within the row, plant them in hills about 3 feet apart.

Give pole beans a structure for support. For example, you could put a 6- to 8-foot stake in the center of each hill. Plant three to four seeds around the stake, about 1 inch deep in the

Source: vic_burton (CC BY-SA 2.0) Source: Living in Monrovia (CC BY-SA 2.0) Source: Chris Winters (CC BY-SA 2.0)

Three types of structures for supporting beans as they grow

soil. As the bean vines mature, they will grow up the stake.

Plant when the soil is moist enough to cause the seeds to germinate and emerge quickly.

Fertilize

Beans grow best when the soil is well fertilized. Spread fertilizer such as 10-20-10 evenly over the area, then mix it in with the top 3 to 4 inches of soil.

Water

In dry weather, water the plants about once a week. Do not let the soil dry out while the beans are blooming, or the blooms will drop and yields will be lower.

Care

Because the roots of beans grow near the soil surface, do not dig too deep when hoeing and pulling weeds, or you'll damage the roots.

After the plants begin to flower and set beans, apply ½ cup of fertilizer for every 10 feet of row. Scatter the fertilizer between the rows. Water the plants after fertilizing.

Diseases

Diseases may be a problem during cool, wet weather. If spots appear on the leaves or bean pods, treat the plant with neem oil, sulfur, or another approved fungicide.

Common diseases and disorders of beans in Texas are anthracnose, iron deficiency, mosaic, powdery mildew, root knot nematodes, root rot, rust, southern blight, and sunscald.

For more information, descriptions, control recommendations, and photos of common vegetable diseases, see the "Diseases" section starting on page 40.

Before using a pesticide, read the label and always follow cautions, warnings, and directions.

Insects

The most common insect pests are aphids, banded cucumber beetles, beet armyworms, cabbage loopers, cutworms, leafhoppers, leafminers, spider mites, and stink bugs.

Photographs, descriptions, and control recommendations for common vegetable insect pests are in the "Insects and other pests" section starting on page 61.

Harvest

Beans are ready to pick when they are about the size of a small pencil.

Source: University of Delaware Carvel REC (CC BY 2.0)

Lima bean pods ready for harvest

For broad, green, and lima beans, harvest when the pods are well filled but have not begun to yellow. Over-mature beans are tough and stringy. Pull them carefully to avoid damaging the plant.

If you pick the beans when they are ready, the plants will continue producing for several weeks.

Store

Keep the harvested beans cold and humid, and use them as soon as possible. Fresh beans can usually be stored for a week in the refrigerator crisper, in plastic bags, or other containers.

Cleanup

To reduce the potential for insect and disease problems next year, remove all the plant material and smooth the bed.

Beets

Best varieties for Texas

- Chioggia
- Detroit Dark Red
- Pacemaker II
- Red Ace
- Ruby Queen

Beets are grown for both the root and top. The tops of any variety can be used for greens when prepared properly.

To prevent the young plants from rotting, use seeds treated with a fungicide.

Choose the site

Plant beets in partial shade and deep, well-drained soils. Because beet roots can reach 36 to 48 inches deep, do not plant them where tree roots will compete.

Beets do best in sandy soil in the spring and heavier clay soil in the fall because sandy soil warms faster than does clay soil. They do not grow well in tight clay.

Prep the soil

Before planting, make sure that the soil is free of rocks, trash, and large sticks.

If your garden soil has a lot of clay, add compost.

Work the soil 8 to 10 inches deep, covering all plant materials with soil so they will break down quickly. The soil should have enough organic matter

Source: signal the police (CC BY-SA 2.0)

Detroit Dark Red, left, and the brighter red Chioggia beets.

to prevent it from crusting, which makes the roots tough.

Beets are also sensitive to soils deficient in boron. Have your soil tested or ask your county Extension agent about boron deficiencies in your area.

Plant

In many South Texas areas, you can grow beets all winter. Farther north, plant them as soon as you can work the soil in the spring. The soil temperature must be at least 40°F for the seeds to sprout.

In poorly drained areas, make the ridges 4 to 6 inches tall to allow water to drain. Then, using a hoe handle, stick, or similar object, make a furrow ½ inch deep down the center of the ridge.

Each beet seed produces 2 to 6 plants. Space the seeds 1 to 2 inches apart in the row. Cover them lightly with loose soil and sprinkle with water.

The plants should sprout up in 7 to 14 days. In hot weather, cover the seeds with sand or light-colored mulch.

For a continuous supply of beets, make several plantings, each 3 weeks apart.

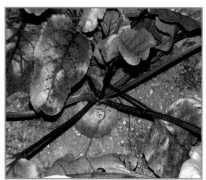
Source: Bff (CC BY-SA 4.0)
Young beet greens

Fertilize

Scatter 1 cup of a complete fertilizer such as 10-20-10 for each 10 feet of row. Mix the fertilizer 4 inches into the soil with a rake and work it into beds.

When the plants are 4 to 6 inches tall, scatter beside them 1 tablespoon of fertilizer for each 10 feet of row.

Water

Water the plants well each week that it does not rain. With enough water, beet root systems can reach 36 inches or more.

Care

Begin thinning the beets as soon as they get crowded in the row. Young tops make excellent greens. After thinning, the plants should be 2 to 3 inches apart.

Keep the beet plants free of weeds. Scratch the soil next to the plants with a rake or hand tool to prevent crusting.

Do not work the soil more than 1 inch deep, or you may injure the roots.

Diseases

Diseases of beets are most severe in cloudy, damp weather. Check the plants daily and treat them with neem oil, sulfur, or another approved fungicide if diseases appear.

Common diseases and problems of beets in Texas are mosaic, powdery mildew, root knot nematodes, and southern blight.

For more information, descriptions, control recommendations, and photos of common vegetable diseases, see the "Diseases" section starting on page 40. Before using a pesticide, read the label and always follow cautions, warnings, and directions.

Insects

The most common insect pests are aphids, banded cucumber beetles, beet armyworms, cabbage loopers, flea beetles, and webworms.

Photographs, descriptions, and control recommendations for common vegetable insect pests are in the "Insects and other pests" section starting on page 61.

Harvest

Beets should be ready to harvest 7 to 8 weeks after planting.

The young, tender tops often have a mild quality, but the greens can be used until they get large and strong flavored.

Harvest the roots when they are the size of a golf ball; if you let them get much bigger, they become woody. To harvest, pull up the plant and cut off the root.

Store

Wash the tops and store them immediately in plastic bags in the refrigerator for 1 or 2 days. The roots will keep 1 to 2 weeks in plastic bags in the refrigerator.

Cleanup

If you don't use all the beets, pull up the plants that are left and place them in a compost pile or spade them into the soil.

Broccoli

Best varieties for Texas

- Arcadia
- Bonanza
- Green Comet
- Green Magic
- Packman
- Premium Crop
- Southern Comet

Choose the site

Broccoli is a cool-season crop that can grow well in most Texas home gardens if the right varieties are planted at the right time.

Broccoli does best with 8 hours of sunlight and in sandy loam soils with lots of organic matter and a pH of 6 to 6.5. The yields at harvest drop if the soil pH is below 6.

Prep the soil

Have your soil tested every 3 to 4 years to determine the nutrients it needs. If you do not have your soil tested, apply about 1 to 2 pounds of a complete fertilizer (such as 10-20-10) for each 100 square feet or about 30 feet of row to be planted.

Add a 3-inch layer of organic matter—such as compost, leaves, or grass clippings—to the garden soil and turn it in a few weeks before planting. This allows it time to decompose and release nutrients into the soil before planting.

Dig the soil as deep as a garden spade or shovel will reach, usually 10 to 12 inches. Turn the organic matter under the soil as soon as possible.

After digging the soil, spread the fertilizer over the soil surface. Then mix it into the soil 2 to 3 inches with a rake or tiller.

Then make beds by pulling the soil into ridges 12 inches wide, 6 to 8 inches high, and 36 inches apart (center to center). This is necessary for good drainage; it also mixes the fertilizer

Packman broccoli

Southern Comet broccoli

into the row where plants can reach it.

Plant

Although you can grow broccoli in both spring and fall, fall planting often is more successful in Texas. Very early spring planting is often delayed by wet or cold weather, and the delay exposes plants to too-hot weather before they mature.

Start with good transplants, which are available at garden centers and online. If you want to grow your own transplants, plant the seeds in peat pots or similar containers about 3 to 4 weeks before transplanting the

fall crop or 6 weeks before the spring crop.

By growing plants from seed, you will have more varieties to select from when you want them. Experienced gardeners plant seed for the fall crop directly into the garden and thin the plants after they come up. You could move any extra plants to other spots in your garden or a neighbor's garden.

Transplant broccoli to the garden according to the dates below (see Texas regions map on page 2).

- **Region 1:** Spring, March 1–April 7; fall, July 15– August 1

- **Region 2:** Spring, February 15–March 20; fall, August 1–20
- **Region 3:** Spring, February 1–March 5; fall, August 20–September 20
- **Region 4:** Spring, January 15–February 20; fall, October 1–20
- **Region 5:** Spring, January 1–February 1; fall, November 1–20

Acclimate the transplants to the cold of early spring or the heat of early fall before transplanting. When properly conditioned, broccoli can survive temperatures as low as 25°F.

Set the transplant in the garden at about the same depth it was in the pot. Broccoli needs 18 to 24 inches between plants and 36 inches between rows. Broccoli spaced too closely will have small heads and fewer side sprouts.

Be sure that the peat pots are moist and not exposed to the air after planting. If you cover broccoli too deep, the stems will rot.

Fertilize

About 4 weeks after transplanting, apply 1 pound of fertilizer for each 30 feet of row beside the plants.

Water the fertilizer into the soil. Another application usually is needed about 4 weeks later. If you use a nitrogen fertilizer such as ammonium nitrate or ammonium sulfate, apply 1 cup per 30 feet of row.

Apply 1 to 2 pounds of a complete fertilizer (such as 10-20-10) for each 100 square feet as the plants grow during the season.

Water

Keep the soil moist but not soaked.

Care

In the spring, mulch with a dark-colored plastic cover or compost. In the fall, use a white

Source: nate steiner (CC BY 2.0)
Broccoli seedling transplant

plastic cover, dried grass clippings, or leaves.

Mulch helps reduce the need for water, controls weeds, and regulates soil temperatures.

To avoid damaging the shallow root system, do not hoe too deep or too close to the plants.

Diseases

These cultural practices can help prevent broccoli diseases:

- Rotate crops every year.
- Do not plant the same crops or crops of the same family in the same place more than once every 3 to 4 years.
- Leave plenty of space between plants to reduce disease problems.

Common diseases and problems of broccoli in Texas are Alternaria leaf spot, black leg, black rot, downy mildew, Fusarium yellow, powdery mildew, root knot nematodes, and southern blight.

For more information, control recommendations, and photos of common vegetable diseases, see the "Diseases" section starting on page 40. Before using a pesticide, read the label and always follow the warnings and directions.

Insects

The most common insect pests are aphids, cabbage loopers, grasshoppers, harlequin bugs, and imported cabbage worms.

Photographs, descriptions, and control recommendations for common vegetable insect pests are in the "Insects and other pests" section starting on page 61.

Harvest

Cut the center heads when the very first flower shows the slightest yellow color. Leave the side sprouts for later harvest.

Source: matsuyuki (CC BY-SA 2.0)
Broccoli ready for harvest

Source: goosmurf (CC BY 2.0)

Rows of broccoli should be 36 inches apart (center to center).

Store

Refrigerate unwashed broccoli in an open plastic bag. Use it within 2 or 3 days.

Cleanup

Follow spring broccoli with summer crops such as southern peas, okra, beans, cucumber, and cantaloupes. Turn the leaves and trimmings from the broccoli under the soil. Compost the large stems.

Brussels sprouts

Best varieties for Texas

- **Diablo**
- **Jade Cross**
- **Royal Marvel**
- **Tasty Nugget**

Choose the site

Brussels sprouts do best in full sunlight and sandy loam soils with plenty of organic matter. Yield drops if the soil pH is below 6.

Prep the soil

A few weeks before planting, dig the soil about 10 to 12 inches deep and add a 3-inch layer of organic matter—such as compost, leaves, or grass clippings—to the soil.

Mix the organic matter into the soil to allow time for the materials time to decompose and release nutrients into the soil before you plant.

Have your soil tested every 3 to 4 years to determine the nutrients it needs. If you do not have your soil tested, apply about 1 to 2 pounds of a complete fertilizer (such as 10-20-10) for each 100 square feet or about 30 feet of row to be planted.

Spread the fertilizer over the soil and then mix it in 2 to 3 inches deep with a rake or tiller.

After fertilizing, make beds by pulling the soil into ridges 12 inches wide, 6 to 8 inches high, and 36 inches apart (center to center). This is necessary for good drainage. It also mixes the fertilizer into the row where the roots can reach it.

Plant

In areas south of Region 2 (see map on page 2), grow Brus-

Source: ErinKhoo (CC BY 2.0)

Brussels sprouts plants

sels sprouts only as a fall crop, because those planted in the spring will not mature before it gets too hot.

Start with healthy transplants, from a nursery or garden center. If you want to grow your own transplants, plant the seeds in peat pots or similar containers about 3 to 4 weeks before transplanting the fall crop or 6 weeks before the spring crop.

By growing plants from seed, you will have more varieties to select from when you want them. Experienced home gardeners plant seed for the fall crop directly into the garden and thin the plants after they come up. Transplant the small plants to other spots in your garden or to a neighbor's garden.

Transplant Brussels sprouts according to the dates below (see the Texas regions map on page 2):

- **Region 1:** Spring, March 1–April 7; fall, July 15–August 1
- **Region 2:** Spring, February 15–March 20; fall, August 1–20
- **Region 3 (northern part):** Spring, February 1–March 5; fall, August 20–Sep. 20
- **Region 4:** Fall, October 1–20
- **Region 5:** Fall, November 1–20

Acclimate the transplants to the cold of early spring or heat of early fall before transplanting. Brussels sprouts can survive 20°F or lower if the temperature drops gradually.

Space the plants 14 to 18 inches apart. Set the transplant in the garden at about the same depth it was in the pot. Be sure that the peat pots are moist and not exposed to air after plant-

Brussels sprouts growing between the leaves and the main stem

ing. If you cover the Brussels sprouts too deeply, the stems will rot.

Fertilize

Apply 1 to 2 pounds of a complete fertilizer (such as 10-20-10) for each 100 square feet as the plants grow during the season.

About 4 weeks after transplanting, apply 1 pound of fertilizer for each 30 feet of row beside the plants.

Water the fertilizer into the soil. Apply more fertilizer about 4 weeks later. If you use nitrogen fertilizer such as ammonium nitrate or ammonium sulfate, apply 1 cup per 30 feet of row.

Water

Keep the soil moist but not soaked.

Care

In the spring, mulch with a dark-colored compost or plastic cover. In the fall, use a white plastic cover, dried grass clippings, or leaves. Mulch helps reduce the need for water, controls weeds, and regulates soil temperatures.

Do not hoe too deep or too close to the plants, or you could damage the shallow root system.

Diseases

Common diseases and problems of Brussels sprouts in Texas are Alternaria leaf spot, black leg, black rot, downy mildew, Fusarium yellow, powdery mildew, root knot nematodes, and southern blight.

For photos and descriptions, see the "Diseases" section starting on page 40.

Source: Nick Saltmarsh (CC BY 2.0)

Harvest Brussels sprouts when they are about 1 inch in diameter.

Insects

The most common insect pests are aphids, cabbage loopers, grasshoppers, harlequin bugs, and imported cabbage worms.

Photographs, descriptions, and control recommendations for common vegetable insect pests are in the "Insects and other pests" section starting on page 61.

Harvest

Sprouts appear between the leaves and the main stem, on the lower leaves first. For best quality, they must have cool weather.

When the lower leaves begin to turn yellow and the sprouts are firm, green, and about 1 inch in diameter, cut off the lower leaves and remove the sprouts with your fingers or a knife. Twist or push the sprout to the side until it snaps.

As you harvest the lower sprouts, you may also remove the yellowing leaves. New sprouts will form higher up the stem as the plant grows.

Harvest Brussels sprouts as soon as they are ready. If you wait too long, they will be tough and of poor quality.

Store

Brussels sprouts will keep for about a week if refrigerated in a plastic bag in the crisper.

Cleanup

Turn the leaves and trimmings from the Brussels sprouts under the soil. Compost the large stems.

You may follow Brussels sprouts planted in the spring with summer crops such as beans, cantaloupes, cucumbers, okra, or peas.

Cabbage

Best varieties for Texas

- Early Jersey Wakefield
- Golden Acre
- Green Boy
- Market Prize
- Rio Verde
- Ruby Ball
- Savoy King
- **Chinese cabbage**
  Brisk Green
  Jade Pagoda
  Michihili
  Monument

Choose the site

Cabbage does best in full sunlight and in sandy loam soils with plenty of organic matter. It prefers soils with a pH of 6 to 6.5; if the pH is below 6, yield drops.

Prep the soil

A few weeks before planting, dig the soil about 10 to 12 inches deep and add a 3-inch layer of organic matter—such as compost, leaves, or grass clippings—to the soil. Mix the organic matter into the soil to allow time for the materials to decompose and release nutrients into the soil before you plant.

Have your soil tested every 3 to 4 years to determine the nutrients it needs. If you do not have your soil tested, apply about 1 to 2 pounds of a complete fertilizer (such as 10-20-10) for each 100 square feet or about 30 feet of row to be

Source: Chrissine Cairns Rios (CC BY 2.0)

Cabbage with mulch for water retention and weed control

Source: Starr Environmental (CC BY 2.0)

Chinese white cabbage, also known as bok choy

planted. Spread the fertilizer over the soil and mix it in 2 to 3 inches deep with a rake or tiller.

After fertilizing, bed the soil by pulling it into ridges 12 inches wide, 6 to 8 inches high, and 36 inches apart (center to center). This is necessary for good drainage. It also mixes the fertilizer into the row where the roots can reach it.

Plant

Although you can grow cabbage in both spring and fall, fall planting often is more successful. Wet or cold weather often delays very early spring planting, and the wait exposes plants to too-hot weather before they mature.

Start with good transplants, which are available from garden centers and online. If you want to grow your own transplants, plant seeds in peat pots or similar containers about 3 to 4 weeks before transplanting the fall crop or 6 weeks before the spring crop.

By growing plants from seed, you will have more varieties to select among. Experienced home gardeners plant seeds for the fall crop directly into the garden and thin the plants after they come up. You could transplant the small plants to other spots in your garden or give them away.

Transplant cabbage to the garden according to the dates below (see map of Texas on page 2):

Region 1: Spring, March 1–April 7; fall, July 15– August 1

Region 2: Spring, February 15–March 20; fall, August 1–20

Region 3: Spring, February 1–March 5; fall, August 20–September 20

Region 4: Spring, January 15–February 20; fall, October 1–20

Region 5: Spring, January

Source: Evelyn Gunn (CC BY-SA 3.0)
Savoy cabbage

1–February 1; fall, November 1–20

Acclimate the transplants to the cold of early spring or heat of early fall before transplanting. Cabbage can survive temperatures as low as 25°F when properly conditioned.

Set the transplant in the garden at about the same depth it was in the pot. Space them 18 to 24 inches between plants and 36 inches between rows.

Be sure that the peat pots are moist and not exposed to the air after planting. If the cabbage is covered too deeply, the stem will rot.

Fertilize

Apply more fertilizer as the plants grow during the season.

Water

Keep the soil moist but not soaked.

Care

In the spring, mulch with compost or a dark-colored plastic. In the fall, use a white plastic cover, dried grass clippings, or leaves. Mulch helps reduce the need for water, controls weeds, and regulates soil temperatures.

Do not hoe too deep or too close to the plants to avoid damaging the shallow root system.

About 4 weeks after transplanting, apply 1 pound of fertilizer for each 30 feet of row beside the plants.

Water the fertilizer into the soil. Another application usually is needed about 4 weeks later. If you use nitrogen fertilizer such as ammonium nitrate

Source: Mark F. Levisay (CC BY 2.0)
Red cabbage almost ready to pick

or ammonium sulfate, apply 1 cup per 30 feet of row.

Diseases

Common diseases and problems of cabbage in Texas are Alternaria leaf spot, black leg, black rot, downy mildew, Fusarium yellow, powdery mildew, root knot nematodes, and southern blight.

For more information, descriptions, control recommendations, and photos of common vegetable diseases, see the "Diseases" section starting on page 40.

Before using a pesticide, read the label and always follow cautions, warnings, and directions.

Insects

The most common insect pests are aphids, banded cucumber beetles, cabbage loopers, grasshoppers, harlequin bugs, and imported cabbage worms.

Photographs, descriptions, and control recommendations for common vegetable insect pests are in the "Insects and other pests" section starting on page 61.

Harvest

To harvest cabbage, cut off the center head about 1 inch down the stem. Harvest when the head becomes firm. Test this by pressing your thumb in the center of the head. The outer leaves should be a uniform green or purple, depending on the type.

Store

Wrap the cabbage head in plastic; you may store it in the refrigerator crisper for up to 2 months.

Cleanup

Turn leaves and trimmings from cabbage crops under the soil. Compost the large stems.

You may follow spring cabbage crops with summer crops such as southern peas, okra, beans, cucumber, and cantaloupes.

Carrots

Best varieties for Texas

- Danvers 126
- Danvers Half Long
- Imperator 58
- Nantes
- Nantes Half Long
- Red Core Chantenay
- Royal Chantenay
- Scarlet Nantes
- Sugar Snax

Choose the site

Carrots do best in loose, well-drained, sandy loam soils. In heavy soils, they mature more slowly, and the roots are often rough and unattractive. They will grow in some shade and do well in small gardens and flower beds.

Prep the soil

Remove all rocks, trash, and large pieces of plant material from the soil surface. Mix in fine pieces of plant material to enrich the soil.

Spade the soil 8 to 12 inches deep. Turn it completely over to cover all the plant material.

Before planting, scatter on the soil 1 cup of a complete fertilizer such as 10-10-10 for each 10 feet of row to be planted. Mix the fertilizer into the soil to 3 to 4 inches deep.

Smooth the soil and make the carrot rows 1 to 2 feet apart. If they are farther apart, plant two rows of carrots on each ridge.

Plant

Begin planting carrots as soon you can work the soil in

Source: kirybabe (CC BY 2.0)
Red Core Chantenay carrots

Source: tamadhanaval (CC BY-SA 2.0)

Carrot seeds take 14 to 21 days to sprout.

the spring. Carrots grow best when it's cool in early spring and late fall. Night temperatures of 55°F and day temperatures of 75°F are ideal. If it's too hot, the carrots will have poor color and low quality.

In South Texas, you can plant carrots any time from July through February. In many South Texas areas, you can grow carrots all winter. For a fall crop in other areas, plant them in August.

Using a hoe handle or stick, make one or two rows ½ inch deep on top of each prepared ridge.

Scatter 18 to 20 seeds per foot in the row. Because carrot seeds take 14 to 21 days to sprout, many gardeners mix a few radish seeds, which sprout quickly, with the carrot seeds to mark the rows.

Cover the seeds lightly.

Fertilize

When the tops are about 4 inches high, scatter 2 tablespoons of fertilizer per 10 feet of row beside the plants.

If the tops become pale, fertilize again when they are 6 to 8 inches tall.

Water

Water the plants as required to keep the soil moist to about 3 inches deep.

Care

When the carrot tops are 4 inches high, thin the plants to 2

Source: sa_ku_ra (CC BY 2.0)

Carrot rows should be 1 to 2 feet apart.

Source: poppet with a camera (CC BY 2.0)

Carrots do best in loose, well-drained soils.

inches apart. Some carrots will be large enough to eat.

As the carrots continue to grow, thin them to 4 inches apart. Overcrowding and rocky soils cause poor-quality roots.

If you mixed radishes with the carrots, pull and eat them as they mature.

To keep the soil from crusting, lightly scratch it around the plants and sprinkle the row with water often, or cover the seeds with vermiculite or sand.

Keep the carrots in your garden free of weeds, especially when they are small.

Diseases

Common diseases and problems of carrots in Texas are black root rot, damping-off, leaf blight, leaf spot, powdery mildew, root knot nematodes, and southern blight.

For more information, descriptions, control recommendations, and photos of common vegetable diseases, see the "Diseases" section starting on page 40. Before using a pesticide, read the label and always follow cautions, warnings, and directions.

Insects

The most common insect pests are cutworms, root maggots, and wireworms.

Photographs, descriptions, and control recommendations for common vegetable insect pests are in the "Insects and

Source: feserc (CC BY 2.0)

Keep the carrots free of weeds.

Source: color line (CC BY 2.0)

Pick carrots while they are still small and succulent.

other pests" section starting on page 61.

Harvest

Carrots should be ready for harvest 70 to 80 days after planting. Harvest when the carrots are small and succulent; always pull the largest carrots in the row.

Pull them from the soil when the roots are 1 to 1½ inches in diameter. To avoid breaking the carrot while pulling, loosen the soil around the carrot with a spade.

To prevent the roots from wilting after harvest, remove the carrot tops and place them in the compost pile.

Store

Remove the tops and wash the carrots before storing them in the bottom of the refrigerator at about 32°F. Carrots will keep for several weeks if you place them in a plastic bag to increase humidity.

Cleanup

Pull up unused carrot plants and toss them in the compost pile or spade them into the soil.

Cauliflower

Best varieties for Texas

- Alverda (green)
- Brocuverde (caul/broc hybrid)
- Imperial
- Majestic
- Snow Crown
- Snowball Y Improved
- Violet Queen (Purple)

Choose the site

Cauliflower does best in full sunlight and sandy loam soils with lots of organic matter. It prefers soils with a pH of 6 to 6.5; if the soil pH is below 6, yield drops.

Prep the soil

A few weeks before planting, dig the soil about 10 to 12 inches deep and add a 3-inch layer of organic matter—such as compost, leaves, or grass clippings—to the soil. Mix the organic matter into the soil to allow time for the materials time to decompose and release nutrients into the soil before you plant.

Have your soil tested every 3 to 4 years to determine the nutrients it needs. If you do not have your soil tested, apply about 1 to 2 pounds of a complete fertilizer (such as 10-20-10) for each 100 square feet or about 30 feet of row to be planted. Spread the fertilizer over the soil and then mix it in

Source: DanTheBeastMan (CC BY-ND 2.0)

A baby cauliflower head

You'll have a greater variety to select from if you grow cauliflower plants from seed.

2 to 3 inches deep with a rake or tiller.

After fertilizing, bed the soil by pulling it into ridges 12 inches wide, 6 to 8 inches high, and 36 inches apart (center to center). This is necessary for good drainage. It also mixes the fertilizer into the row where the roots can reach it.

Plant

Although you can grow cauliflower in both spring and fall, fall planting often is more successful. Very early spring planting is often delayed by wet or cold weather, and the delay exposes plants to too-hot weather before they mature.

Start with good transplants from a nursery or garden center. If you want to grow your own transplants, plant seeds in peat pots or similar containers about 3 to 4 weeks before transplanting the fall crop or 6 weeks before the spring crop.

By growing plants from seed, you will have more varieties to select from when you want them. Experienced home gardeners plant seed for the fall crop directly into the garden and thin the plants after they come up. Transplant the extra plants to other spots.

Transplant cauliflower according to the dates below (see map of Texas regions on page 2):

Region 1: Spring, March 1– April 7; fall, July 15– August 1

Region 2: Spring, February 15–March 20; fall, August 1–20

Region 3: Spring, February 1–March 5; fall, August 20–September 20

Region 4: Spring, January 15–February 20; fall, October 1–20

Region 5: Spring, January 1–February 1; fall, November 1–20

Acclimate the transplants to the cold of early spring or heat of early fall before transplant-

Source: Rob_moments (CC BY 2.0)

A cauliflower seedling

ing. Space them 18 to 24 inches between plants and 36 inches between rows.

Set the transplant in the garden at about the same depth it was in the pot. Be sure that the peat pots are moist and not exposed to air after planting. If you cover the cauliflower too deeply, the stems will rot.

To take advantage of the extra space in the rows, you could plant radishes or greens between the young cauliflower plants.

Fertilize

Apply 1 to 2 pounds of a complete fertilizer (such as 10-20-10) for each 100 square feet as the plants grow during the season.

Water

Keep the soil moist but not soaked.

Care

In the spring, mulch with a dark-colored plastic cover or compost. In the fall, use a white plastic cover, dried grass clippings, or leaves in the fall.

Mulch helps reduce the need for water, controls weeds, and regulates soil temperatures. Do not hoe too deep or too close to the plants to avoid damaging the shallow root system.

About 4 weeks after transplanting, apply 1 pound of fertilizer for each 30 feet of row beside the plants.

Water the fertilizer into the soil. Another application usually is needed about 4 weeks later. If you use nitrogen fertilizer such as ammonium nitrate or ammonium sulfate, apply 1 cup per 30 feet of row.

When the cauliflower head can be seen easily, gather the

Source: Linda N. (CC BY 2.0)

A maturing cauliflower plant

Source: Bruce and Patty Leander

Cauliflower with the leaves tied over the head (blanched)

longest leaves together over the head and tie them with a rubber band, soft twine, or clothes pin. This is called blanching. It shades the head and prevents it from becoming yellowish green.

Check the plants often for insect damage after blanching. The head should be ready to harvest in 8 to 10 days.

Diseases

Common diseases and problems of cauliflower in Texas are Alternaria leaf spot, black leg, black rot, downy mildew, Fusarium yellow, powdery mildew, root knot nematodes, and southern blight.

To help keep disease pressure down:

- Rotate crops every year.
- Do not plant the same crops or crops of the same family in the same place more than once every 3 to 4 years.
- Leave plenty of space between plants to reduce disease problems.

For more information, descriptions, control recommendations, and photos of common vegetable diseases, see the "Diseases" section starting on page 40. Before using a pesticide, read the label and always follow cautions, warnings, and directions.

Insects

The most common insect pests are aphids, cabbage loopers, grasshoppers, harlequin bugs, and imported cabbage worms.

Photographs, descriptions, and control recommendations for common vegetable insect pests are in the "Insects and other pests" section starting on page 61.

Harvest

Cut the center heads when they are tight. Overly mature heads become open and loose, and flowers begin to open.

Harvest cauliflower as soon as it is ready. Delayed harvest results in tough, poor-quality produce.

Store

Chill cauliflower immediately after harvest. Refrigerate it unwashed in a paper or plastic bag for up to a week.

Cleanup

Follow spring cauliflower with summer crops such as southern peas, okra, beans, cucumber, and cantaloupes.

Turn the leaves and trimmings from the cauliflower under the soil. Compost the large stems.

Corn

Best varieties for Texas

There are three major types of sweet corn: standard, super-sweet, and sugar-enhanced. They differ in sweetness, harvest and storage periods, and germination rates.

Standard varieties have the traditional flavor and texture of sweet corn, but the quality keeps for only 1 to 2 days in the garden, and they don't store well because the sugar quickly converts to starch. Varieties to plant:

- Bonanza
- Merit
- Silver Queen
- Sweet G-90

Sugar-enhanced corn has a higher sugar content and is more tender than standard sweet corn. Varieties to plant:

- Ambrosia
- Argent
- Bodacious
- Golden Queen
- Kandy Korn
- Legend
- Tendertreat

Supersweet varieties have the highest sugar content and the longest harvest and storage periods. However, they are slow to germinate, and the kernels are tougher than those of the other types. Varieties to plant:

- Crisp-N-Sweet
- Florida Staysweet
- Frontier
- Honey n Pearl
- How Sweet It Is
- Mirai
- Summer Sweet

Popcorn
- Robust White
- Strawberry

Choose the site

Corn can tolerate many soil types but prefers well-drained soils with a pH between 5.5 and 7.0. In a sandy or low-pH soil, it may suffer from magnesium deficiency.

Like most vegetables, corn grows best in areas with plenty of sunlight.

Prep the soil

Before planting, remove weeds, rocks, and trash, and work the top 8 to 10 inches of soil. Work the soil only when it is dry enough not to stick to garden tools.

Fertilize

Use 2 to 3 pounds of fertilizer, such as 10-10-10, for every 100 square feet of garden area. Spread the fertilizer evenly over the soil and then work it into the soil 3 to 4 inches deep.

Rake the soil to smooth the surface.

Plant

Sweet corn is a warm-season crop; plant it after the soil warms and there is no more danger of frost. If you have room, plant again when the first corn plants have three to five

Source: zayzayem (CC BY-SA 2.0)

Corn planted in several rows to enhance pollination

leaves. This usually takes 2 to 3 weeks.

You will need 1 to 2 ounces of seed for every 100 feet of row. Seed saved from last year's sweet corn will not grow a good crop.

Plant corn in several short rows instead of one long row. This makes it easier for the corn plants to pollinate, which is necessary for ears of corn to have plump, juicy kernels.

Plant the corn seeds about 1 inch deep and 3 to 4 inches apart in the row. Space the rows 2½ to 3 feet apart. After the plants are up, thin them to 1 foot apart. If you plant them closer, the ears will be small and poorly filled.

Water

Water the corn as needed to keep it from wilting. Especially when the kernels are forming, make sure it has enough water.

Care

Hoe or till the soil just under the surface. When weeding, hoe just below the soil surface. Deep hoeing will cut the corn roots, which are close to the top of the soil.

When the plants are about 2 feet tall, apply 1 cup of fertilizer for every 10 feet of garden row. Scatter the fertilizer evenly between the rows and mix it lightly with the soil. Water after fertilizing.

Diseases

Common diseases of corn in Texas are common rust, downy mildew, northern leaf blight, and smut.

If a few of your corn plants are stunted, they may have a viral disease. Remove them to keep the virus from spreading.

For more information, descriptions, control recommendations, and photos of common vegetable diseases, see the "Diseases" section starting on page 40.

Source: AtHandGuides.com (CC BY 2.0)

Corn is ready for harvest when the silk on the ears has turned dark brown.

Before using a pesticide, read the label and always follow cautions, warnings, and directions.

Insects

The most common insect pests are banded cucumber beetles, beet armyworms, fall armyworms, flea beetles, corn earworms, cutworms, European corn borers, fall armyworms, flea beetles, grasshoppers, stink bugs, and wireworms.

Photographs, descriptions, and control recommendations for common vegetable insect pests are in the "Insects and other pests" section starting on page 61.

Source: timsackton (CC BY-SA 2.0)
Popcorn plants

Harvest

Corn is ready for harvest about 3 weeks after the tassel grows on top of the corn plant. It is ripe when the juice from the kernels is milky white, the silk on the ears has turned dark brown, the ears are firm, and the kernels on the tips of the unhusked ears are plump and milky.

Sweet corn is not ready when the juice of the kernel is watery. It is overripe when the kernels get large, chewy, and pasty like dough.

The best time to pick corn is in the early morning or evening when it is cool. To harvest the ears, hold the stalk below the ear and twist the tip of the ear toward the ground until it breaks off.

Store

Because sweet corn converts from sugar to starch very rapidly, cook or chill it immediately after harvest.

Store corn in the husk. Place it uncovered in the refrigerator for 1 or 2 days. Corn stored for more than 2 days loses its sweetness.

Cleanup

Reduce insect and disease problems next year by removing all the plant material and smoothing the bed.

Note: Old corn plants make good compost for garden soil. They break down much faster if you shred them before composting.

Cucumbers

Best varieties for Texas

- **Pickling**
  Calypso
  Carolina
  Fancypak
  Multipik
  National Pickling
- **Slicing**
  Burpless
  Dasher II
  Poinsett
  Pointsett 76
  Slice Master
  Straight 8
  Sweet Slice
  Sweet Success

Choose the site

Cucumber vines need a lot of space. They can reach 6 to 8 feet long or more and are best suited to larger gardens, where they can spread out on the ground. However, they can grow in small areas if the plants are caged or trellised.

Although cucumbers do best in loose sandy loam soil, they can also grow in any well-drained soil. They must have full sunlight.

Because their roots reach 36 to 48 inches deep, do not plant them where tree roots will rob them of water and nutrients.

Prep the soil

Remove all rocks, large sticks, and trash. Turn under the small, fine pieces of plant material to enrich the soil.

Source: fortherock (CC BY-SA 2.0)
Caged cucumber plants

Source: Doug Beckers (CC BY-SA 2.0) Source: poppet with a camera (CC BY 2.0)

Cucumbers supported by a bamboo and wire trellis (left) and a metal trellis

Spade the soil to 8 to 12 inches deep. Turn each shovel of soil completely over to cover all plant materials with soil.

Work the soil into beds 4 to 6 inches high and at least 36 inches apart. Ridges are especially important in heavy soils and poorly drained areas because cucumbers must have good drainage.

Plant

Cucumbers must grow in warm weather and cannot survive frost. Do not plant them until all danger of frost has passed and the soil begins to warm.

Use a hoe or stick to make a small furrow about 1 inch deep down the center of each ridge. Drop three or four seeds in groups every 12 to 14 inches down the row. By planting several seeds, you are more likely to get a stand.

Cover the seeds with about 1 inch of fine soil. Use the flat side of a hoe to firm the soil over the seeds, but do not pack it.

To save space, plant fast-maturing crops such as lettuce and radishes between the cucumber hills. They will be ready for harvest before the cucumber vines get too large.

If your garden is small, plant three or four seeds in hills 4 to 6 inches high along a trellis or wire.

Fertilize

Cucumbers need plenty of fertilizer. Scatter 1 cup of a complete fertilizer such as 10-10-10 or 10-20-10 for each 10 feet of row; then work the fertilizer into the soil and leave the surface smooth.

When the vines are about 10 to 12 inches long, apply about ½ cup of fertilizer for each 10 feet of row or 1 tablespoon per plant.

Water

Soak the plants well with water every week if it does not rain.

Care

Thin the plants soon after they sprout.

Keep the cucumbers as weed-free as possible. Do not plow or hoe the soil deeper than about 1 inch because you may cut the feeder roots and slow the plant's growth.

Cucumbers produce two kinds of flowers, male and female. Male flowers open first and always drop off. Female flowers form the cucumber and should not drop off.

If the female flowers do begin to drop off, touch the inside of each male and female

Source: Nadia Talent (CC BY 2.0)   Source: Rasbak (GFDL or CC BY-SA 3.0)

Female cucumber flowers (left) form the cucumber; male cucumber flowers (right) bloom first and always drop off.

flower with a soft brush or cotton swab. This will pollinate the flowers and help them develop into fruit.

Diseases

Several diseases attack cucumbers; initial symptoms are usually spots on the upper or lower sides of the leaves or on the fruit.

Common diseases of cucumbers in Texas are Alternaria leaf spot, anthracnose, bacterial wilt, blossom-end rot, downy mildew, Fusarium wilt, powdery mildew, sooty mold, squash leaf curl, and yellow vine.

Check the plants daily and spray them with an approved fungicide if diseases appear. Neem oil, sulfur, and other fungicides are available for use.

For more information, descriptions, control recommendations, and photos of common vegetable diseases, see the "Diseases" section starting on page 40. Before using a pesticide, read the label and always follow cautions, warnings, and directions.

Insects

The most common insect pests are aphids, banded cucumber beetles, cabbage loopers, leafminers, spotted cucumber beetles, and squash bugs.

Photographs, descriptions, and control recommendations for common vegetable insect pests are in the "Insects and other pests" section starting on page 61.

Harvest

Harvest when the cucumbers are bright, firm, and green and before they get too large. Do not wait until they turn yellow. Yellow cucumbers are over mature and will have strong flavor.

Harvest sweet pickles at 1½ to 2 inches long, and dills when they are 3 to 4 inches long, bright green, and less crisp.

Store

Refrigerate cucumbers in the crisper for no more than 5 days.

Cleanup

To reduce the potential for insect and disease problems next year, remove all the plant material and smooth the bed.

Eggplant

Best varieties for Texas

- Black Bell
- Black Magic
- Epic
- Classic
- Florida High Bush
- Florida Market
- Night Shadow

Oriental varieties:

- Ichibon
- Tycoon

Choose the site

Eggplant prefers fertile, well-drained, sandy loam soils with a pH between 5.5 and 7.2.

Prep the soil

Remove all weeds, and till the soil to loosen it to a depth of 6 to 10 inches. Incorporate a 3- to 4-inch layer of compost if possible.

Plant

Although you can seed eggplant directly into the garden, beginning gardeners may find it is easier to use transplants.

If you can't find the varieties you want in garden centers, start seeds 6 to 8 weeks before they are to be transplanted outside. Grow the seeds indoors. They will germinate in 5 days if kept at 86°F, but could take up to 14 days at 65°F.

Eggplant is a tropical plant, so it is very sensitive to cold;

Source: Nostepinne (CC BY 2.0)

Eggplant blossoms

Source: woodleywonderworks (CC BY 2.0)

Row of eggplants with first fruits

don't plant it outside until all risk of frost has passed and daytime temperatures are at least 65°F.

Because the plants will grow to 2 to 4 feet, space them 24 to 36 inches apart.

Fertilize

Eggplant needs a consistent supply of nutrients. It is best to get a soil test and follow its recommendations.

If no soil test is conducted, add a total of 2 to 3 pounds of a complete fertilizer (6-12-12, 10-10-10, or 9-16-16) per 1,000 square feet. Apply half the fertilizer before planting and the other half after the first fruits appear.

After transplanting the eggplant, pour ¼ cup of starter solution around each plant. Make a starter solution by dissolving 2 tablespoons of a complete fertilizer in 1 gallon of water.

Water

Eggplant also needs consistent water, at least 1 inch per week. It is better to give one thorough soaking than several frequent, short waterings, because frequent watering promotes shallow roots.

Weather and soil type, of course, will affect water demand. High temperatures, high winds, and sandy soils increase the need for water.

Care

Keep weeds under control because they compete with plants for water, nutrients, and light. Use mulch to conserve soil moisture and reduce weed competition.

Diseases

Quite a few diseases can damage eggplant at various stages, including Alternaria leaf spot, anthracnose, damping-off, early blight, late blight, leaf spot, Phytophthora blight, and Verticillium wilt.

Prevent diseases by planting resistant varieties, rotating

crops, using proper irrigation and plant spacing, and practicing good sanitation (such as disposing of diseased plants).

For more information, descriptions, control recommendations, and photos of common vegetable diseases, see the "Diseases" section starting on page 40.

Before using a pesticide, read the label and always follow cautions, warnings, and directions.

Insects

The most common insect pests are beet armyworms, eggplant flea beetles, flea beetles, Colorado potato beetles, cutworms, leafhoppers, leafminers, spider mites, and stink bugs.

Photographs, descriptions, and control recommendations

Source: BinaryApe (CC BY 2.0)
Container-grown eggplants

for common vegetable insect pests are in the "Insects and other pests" section starting on page 61.

Harvest

Eggplants are ready for harvest when they are one-third to full size and about 6 to 8 inches in diameter but still firm with bright color. Harvest before the skin becomes dull and the seeds become hard.

A general rule is that the fruit is ready to be picked if you lightly press the side of the fruit with your thumbnail and the indention stays.

Although you could break the eggplant off the plant, it is better for the plant if the fruit is cut off. Beware of the spines on the fruit stem; they can hurt an ungloved hand. Handle the harvested fruit gently so they aren't bruised.

Store

Eggplant can be refrigerated for about a week.

Cleanup

To reduce the potential for insect and disease problems next year, remove all the plant material and smooth the bed.

Garlic

Best varieties for Texas

- California Early
- California Softneck
- Elephant Garlic
- French Mild Silverskin
- Mexican Purple
- New York White

Choose the site

Garlic grows best in full sun and in well-drained sandy or clay loams with a pH range of 6.0 to 8.4. However, it will adapt to a broad range of soil types if you manage it well.

Don't plant garlic on a site where onions or another member of the Lily family has grown in recent years.

Prep the soil

Garlic needs good drainage and lots of organic matter. Use raised beds if your soil has a high clay content or drains poorly.

Before planting, apply fertilizer according to the soil test recommendations. If you don't have soil test results, mix in about 5 pounds of a 10 percent nitrogen fertilizer (such as 10-10-10) per 100 square feet. Then work in some compost or well-rotted manure.

Plant

Plant garlic in the fall for harvest the following spring. At planting, the soil temperature at 2 inches deep needs to be less than 85°F.

Source: Linda N. (CC BY 2.0)

If your soil drains poorly or has a high clay content, plant the garlic in a raised bed.

Garlic needs cool conditions during the growing season. Temperatures below 40°F for 6 to 8 weeks are required for vernalization, which is the promotion of flowering by cool weather.

Once vernalized, the plants begin forming bulbs when the days become longer than 13 hours and the soil warms to more than 60°F.

Plant each clove separately, pointed-side up, about 1 inch deep, and 3 to 4 inches apart. For elephant garlic, plant 2 to 4 cloves per foot of bed.

Add mulch after planting to discourage weed growth.

Fertilize

In the spring, add a nitrogen fertilizer when the plants are 6 to 8 inches tall.

Water

Make sure that the garlic gets 1 to 2 inches of water per week from the time it begins growing quickly in the spring until it matures, or the tops turn yellow. Stop watering once the cloves are well filled, the bulb has reached the size you want, and three to five well-formed scales surround the bulbs.

Source: oatsy40 (CC BY 2.0)
Garlic in flower

The cloves will rot if the soil is waterlogged.

Care

Because garlic does not compete well, keep weeds under control, especially during the first 2 months of growth.

Some types of garlic produce flowers, robbing the plant of energy. To redirect the energy to the bulb, cut off the flower stalk.

Diseases

Common diseases of garlic in Texas are botrytis rot, downy mildew, pink root, powdery mildew, purple blotch, and white rot.

For more information, descriptions, control recommendations, and photos of common garlic diseases, see the "Diseases" section starting on page 40.

Source: Tony Austin (CC BY 2.0)

Garlic is ready to harvest when the tops turn yellow and fall over.

Dry garlic by hanging it up in a well-ventilated area.

Before using a pesticide, read the label and always follow the warnings and directions.

Insects

The most common insect pests are armyworms, cutworms, mites, and thrips.

Photos, descriptions, and control recommendations for common vegetable insect pests are in the "Insects and other pests" section starting on page 61.

Harvest

Garlic is mature and ready to harvest when the tops begin to turn yellow and fall over.

Dry the garlic thoroughly after harvest, and hang it up in a well-ventilated area to prevent rot. Before storing it, remove the tops and roots. Do not expose it to extremely high or low temperatures after harvest.

Store

Store garlic at about 75°F. It should keep for 6 to 8 months if you store it in a dry, well-ventilated area.

Cleanup

Do not plant onions after garlic in the same spot.

Greens

Best varieties for Texas

- **Collards**
  Blue Max
  Champion
  Flash
  Georgia LS
  Georgia Southern
  Top Bunch
  Vates

- **Kale**
  Dwarf Blue Curled
    Scotch
  Dwarf Blue Curled Vates
  Green Curled
  Rebor

- **Lettuce**
  Butterhead/Bibb
    Buttercrunch
    Ermosa
    Esmeralda
    Summer Bibb

Crisphead/iceberg
  Classic
  Mission
  Prizehead
Looseleaf
  Black Seeded Simpson
  Brunia Red
  Crawford Reseeding
  Green Ice
  Lolla Rossa
  Oakleaf
  Red Fire
  Red Sails
  Redina
  Ruby Red
  Salad Bowl
  Simpson Elite
  Tango
  Vulcan Red
Romaine
  Freckles
  Giant Caesar
  Little Caesar

Romaine
- Parris Island
- Plato II
- Valmaine

- **Mustard**
- Early Mizuna
- Florida Broadleaf
- Green Wave
- Large Smooth Leaf
- Southern Giant Curled
- Tender Green

- **Spinach**
- Bloomsdale
- Melody
- Space
- Tyee

- **Swiss chard**
- Bright Lights
- Fordhook Giant
- Lucullus
- Rhubarb Chard
- Rhubarb Red
- Ruby

- **Turnips**
  Greens
  - Alamo
  - All Top
  - Seven Top
  - Shogoin
  - Topper

Roots
- Globe
- Just Right Hybrid
- Purple Top
- Royal
- Royal Crown
- Tokyo Cross
- White Globe
- White Lady

- **Other specialty greens**
- Malabar spinach
- Molokhia
- New Zealand spinach
- Pak choi
- Radicchio
- Tatsoi

Molokhia, Malabar, and New Zealand spinach are good substitutes for spinach during hot weather, as they tolerate high temperatures but not cold. However, the seeds are slow to germinate.

Choose the site

Collards need deep soil that drains well and as much sun as possible.

Lettuces prefer deep, well-drained, black sandy loams with a pH 6 to 7.6; they can tolerate a wide range of soils from fairly sandy (spring planting) to heavy clays (fall planting). They will not tolerate acid soils.

Source: photofarmer (CC BY 2.0)

Butterhead mini lettuce

Raised beds are ideal for lettuce because:

- The soil is less likely to be compacted.
- Diseases are less prevalent.
- It is easier to manage the water levels in the soil.

If possible, plant **mustard** and **turnips** in full sun. For best production, they also need well-drained soil. The greens are also easily grown in window boxes and containers on an apartment balcony or patio.

Mustard works well as a border to a flowerbed or sidewalk. Both the broadleaf and curled leaf varieties are attractive and add green to a flowerbed.

Spinach and most other greens grow best in well-drained soil with lots of organic matter. They prefer full sunlight but will tolerate partial shade.

Prep the soil

Before planting, remove rocks and large sticks from the soil; then spade it over to cover the plant material on the soil surface. Allow time for the material to begin rotting.

Add organic matter if the soil is mostly clay or light sand. This is vital if you are growing the turnips for the roots; heavy soil can cause the roots to be rough and poorly shaped. A 4-inch layer of compost is enough. Spread the compost over the planting area before digging.

Because **spinach** has a deep taproot, the soil must be worked at least 8 to 10 inches deep. Dig the soil in the early spring when it is dry enough not

Source: OakleyOriginals (CC BY 2.0)

Spinach

to stick to garden tools. Break up large clods, and remove the trash and weeds.

The roots of a **collard** plant easily reach 2 feet deep or more. Dig the soil as deep as possible or at least 10 to 12 inches. This will loosen the soil so the small feeder roots can grow more easily.

Work the soil into planting beds about 4 inches high.

Just before planting, add fertilizer according to soil test results. Or, scatter a complete garden fertilizer such as 10-10-10 over the area. Use 2 or 3 pounds per 100 square feet, or about 1 cup for each 10 feet of row.

Use a rake to mix the fertilizer 3 to 4 inches into the soil.

Source: Steven Jackson Photography (CC BY 2.0)

Collard leaf

Work the soil into ridges 6 to 8 inches high and at least 36 inches apart. This will bring the fertilizer under the row, where the plants can reach it easily. The ridges also allow water to drain away from the plant roots.

Plant

Start greens from transplants or from seeds sown directly in the garden. Plant them as soon as you can work the soil in the spring, or in August or later in the fall. The hot weather and long days of summer cause spinach to "bolt," or produce a seed stalk that makes it unusable for food.

Instead of planting all at once, space the plantings 10 to 14 days apart. This is called *succession planting*. It distributes your harvest evenly over a few weeks rather than having all the harvest at once.

To grow more plants per square foot, plant greens in one big block rather than in rows by spreading the seeds on a bed 18 to 20 inches wide and covering them with soil. However, this method makes it harder to control weeds because you have to pull them by hand.

For fall crops, it's vital that the seeds be planted in moist soil. Cover the seeds lightly with soft soil or compost; then sprinkle the row with water to speed sprouting. Do not let the soil dry out. Regular overhead watering helps seedlings survive early germination and get established.

Another option is to cover the seeds with sand or light-colored mulch to keep the row cool. Sprinkle the row regularly with water to prevent soil crusting until the small plants break through.

Under good conditions, most of the plants should be up in 3 to 7 days. Add mulch to help conserve water and control weeds.

Collards, mustard, and **turnips:** Transplants are usually used for the spring crop. They add 4 to 5 weeks to the growing season because you can grow them indoors before the weather is warm enough to plant the seeds outside.

Collard seeds sprout when the soil temperature reaches 45°F; turnips and mustard seeds will sprout if the soil temperature is 40°F or higher.

Move the transplants into the garden in the spring as soon

Source: Get Ahead (CC BY 2.0)

Turnip greens

as you can work the soil; in most of Texas, this is in February or March.

For a fall crop, start planting about 80 days before frost, which corresponds to August or September in most areas of Texas. Seed them heavily and then thin them. In South Texas and coastal areas, greens grow well all winter.

Set the plants in the soil at about the same depth as they grew indoors. Space them 18 to 24 inches apart in the row. Water the plants after transplanting.

When planting seeds, make a shallow furrow about ½ inch deep in the center of the bed. Scatter the seeds lightly in the furrow.

With a little practice, you can easily scatter the seeds by using your fingers to lightly tap the edge of the open seed packet. One teaspoon of seed will plant about 30 feet of row.

Cover the seeds with about ¼ inch of loose soil or compost; then sprinkle them with water. The plants should come up in 6 to 12 days. However, the colder the soil is, the more slowly the seeds will sprout.

Plant **kale** in early spring or late fall. It is sometimes called "flowering cabbage" and makes a good border for flower beds or sidewalks.

Use a hoe handle, stick, or similar tool to make planting furrows about ½ inch deep and 1½ to 2 feet apart down the bed. Plant seeds about 1 inch apart down the row and cover with loose soil or compost. For the fall crop, cover with sand or other light-colored material to reflect heat and keep the soil cooler.

Malabar is a vining plant; plant it next to a fence or trellis for support, with 10 to 12 inches between plants.

Plant **New Zealand spinach** in rows 3 feet apart and thin to 2 feet between plants.

Swiss chard is sometimes called summer spinach, but it is actually a member of the beet family and tastes like beet greens. Swiss chard is very tolerant of heat and light freezes and can be harvested all year in many areas of Texas.

Fertilize

Greens grow best when given plenty of fertilizer. Fertilize as directed by a soil test report. Mix the fertilizer about 3 inches into the soil.

About 3 weeks after germination, apply ¼ to ⅓ cup of fertilizer for every 10 feet of row. Mix the fertilizer lightly with the soil, and water the plants.

When the plants are thinned to their final spacing or if they become pale green, add a little more fertilizer. Collards need plenty

Source: naturalflow (CC BY-SA 2.0)

Kale

Source: Macleay Grass Man (CC BY 2.0)
New Zealand spinach

of nitrogen to develop their dark green leaf color.

You may need to add fertilizer again along the side of the rows in 4 to 6 weeks if they become pale and there is no sign that insects caused the change.

Water

Water the plants well each week if it does not rain. Water them thoroughly, and do not allow them to wilt. You will need to water more often if the weather is hot or the soil is sandy.

When watering, soak the soil thoroughly to encourage the roots to grow deeper into the soil, which helps them withstand dry periods better.

For lettuces, avoid excessive moisture just before the head matures, as it can cause puffiness or soft heads.

Care

Keep the plants free of weeds, especially when they are small, because weeds use water and nutrients that the growing crop needs. Hand-pull weeds close to the plants so that hoeing won't cut vegetable roots and cause the plants to wilt.

Collards: Let the plants grow until they are about 4 to 6 inches tall or become crowded in the row. Then thin the plants gradually until about 18 inches remain between them. Crowding causes the leaves to be smaller and paler.

Transplant the thinned plants to another spot or use them as greens.

Lettuces: Because the root systems are shallow, lettuce plants compete poorly with weeds for nutrients and water. For the best quality and yield, pull weeds and keep the soil uniformly moist.

Mustard and turnips: When the plants become crowded in the row, thin them by pulling some plants. Small plants of both turnips and mustard make delicious greens.

Source: jessicareeder (CC BY 2.0)

Red mustard greens

Thin the mustard plants until they are about 6 inches apart. Leave the turnips 3 to 4 inches apart; remember that overcrowding prevents the turnip roots from developing.

Turnips and mustards need adequate nitrogen to develop a dark green color. When the plants are 4 to 5 inches tall, apply ½ cup of fertilizer for each 10 feet of row. Spread the fertilizer beside the plants, mix it lightly with the soil, and water it into the soil.

If the soil is sandy and the season is wet, apply more fertilizer later.

Spinach and other greens: After the plants come up and become crowded in the row, begin thinning them. Leave kale plants 1 foot apart, chard 6 inches apart, and spinach 3 to 4 inches apart.

Do not throw away thinned plants, as they make excellent tender greens.

About 30 days after the plants come up, scatter ¼ cup of garden fertilizer beside the plants for every 10 feet of row and water thoroughly.

Diseases

Common diseases and problems of greens in Texas are Alternaria leaf spot, anthracnose, bacterial leaf spot, black rot, damping-off, downy mildew, mosaic virus, root knot nematodes, turnip mosaic, and white rust.

The leaves of spinach, turnips, and mustard often show some disease damage in cool, damp weather. Do not plant spinach in the same place in your garden more than once every 2 or 3 years.

If the plants have spots on the leaves, you may need to use a fungicide. Check the plants daily, and if diseases appear, treat them with a fungicide approved for collards, such as neem oil or sulfur.

Before applying any pesticide, always read the label. Follow cautions, warnings, and directions and observe waiting periods between spray applications and harvest.

For more information, descriptions, control recommendations, and photos of common diseases of greens, see the "Diseases" section starting on page 40.

Insects

The most common insect pests of greens are aphids, beet armyworms, cabbage loopers, cucumber beetles, cutworms, grasshoppers, harlequin bugs, leafhoppers, leafminers, imported cabbage worms, root maggots, and thrips.

Photographs, descriptions, and control recommendations for common vegetable insect pests are in the "Insects and

Source: pause.reflect (CC BY 2.0)

Harvest the lower leaves of kale as the plant grows.

other pests" section starting on page 61.

Harvest

For **chard** and **kale**, harvest the lower leaves as they grow. These plants also will continue growing.

Collards can be harvested in two ways:

For small plants that need thinning, cut the entire plant about 4 inches above the ground. Sometimes they will sprout back from the side of the stem.

For larger plants, harvest the lower leaves of collards. Break off the outer leaves when they are 6 to 10 inches long and before they start to yellow. This allows the plant to continue growing and producing more leaves. Avoid wilted leaves.

Source: eren (sea+prairie) (CC BY 2.0)

Swiss chard

Source: joi (CC BY 2.0)

Romaine lettuce

Source: AZAdam (CC BY-SA 2.0)

Radicchio

In mild regions, such as South Texas and coastal areas, collards will produce all winter. Collards can stand temperatures of 20°F or less in some cases. They taste sweeter after a light frost.

For leaf **lettuce**, snap off the mature outer leaves as you need them. Harvest heads of lettuce while they are still firm, using a sharp knife to make a clean cut through the stem below the head.

Harvest **spinach** when the plants are 6 to 8 inches tall. In the spring, pull up the entire plant because it stops producing in hot weather.

For the fall crop, clip the leaves just above the crown about 1 to 2 inches above ground level. If you water and fertilize lightly, the plants will continue growing.

Harvest the tips of **Malabar spinach** plants when they are 3 to 4 inches long.

Mustard and **turnip** greens are good until the weather gets hot. Too much heat causes them to be tough and strong flavored.

Harvest mustard greens when they are young and tender. Cut the large outer leaves and leave the inner leaves to continue growing. You can also cut and use the entire plants.

Most turnip varieties produce greens in 40 days. Turnip roots generally take 50 to 60 days to produce.

Harvest turnip greens by pulling up the entire plant when the leaves are 4 to 6 inches long. Harvest the roots when they are 2 to 2½ inches in diameter. If left longer, they will get tough and stringy.

Both mustards and turnips lose quality and go to seed quickly when days grow long and hot. Do not leave them in the garden too long.

Store

Refrigerate spinach and most other greens unwashed in a closed plastic bag for no more than 2 to 3 days. Collards can last 3 to 5 days. Wait to wash them until you are ready to use them.

Lettuces are extremely perishable. Refrigerate them immediately after harvest.

Turnip roots will keep several weeks in a cool, humid area such as a root cellar or the bottom of the refrigerator.

Cleanup

To reduce the potential for insect and disease problems next year, remove all the plant material and smooth the bed.

Unused leafy vegetables make good additions to a compost pile. They break down quickly and can be turned into the garden soil.

Melons

Best varieties for Texas

- **Cantaloupe (muskmelon)**
  Ambrosia
  Caravelle
  Hale's Best
  Israeli
  Magnum 45
  Mainstream
  Mission
  Perlita
  TAM Uvalde

- **Honeydew**
  Honey Girl
  Sweet Delight
  TAM Dew

- **Seedless watermelon**
  Tiffany
  Tri-X 313

- **Watermelon**
  Allsweet

Black Diamond
Charleston Gray
Crimson Sweet
Jubilee
Mickylee
Mirage
Royal Jubilee
Tendersweet

In the United States, muskmelons are often called cantaloupes. However, the true cantaloupe is a small, warty fruit and is not usually grown here.

Choose the site

Because melons are vining crops that require a lot of space, they should be grown only in large gardens. You can grow cantaloupes in a small garden if you trellis the vines and support the fruit.

Melons grow best on a deep, well-drained, sandy or sandy

Source: jbolles (CC BY-SA 2.0)   Source: BarnyardBBS (CC BY 2.0)

In small gardens, some types of melons can be grown on trellises and the fruit supported by such materials as nylon hosiery (left) or a net sling.

loam soil with plenty of organic matter. Heavy soils with a lot of clay often cause small, weak plants that produce fewer melons. Melons prefer soils with a neutral pH, and if the soil is too acidic, the plants will drop their blossoms.

Prep the soil

Dig or plow the soil 8 to 10 inches deep in winter or early spring. If you add organic matter or manure, it should be well composted.

Apply manure or compost at 50 to 100 pounds per 1,000 square feet, or about 2 to 4 tons per acre, to build the organic matter content of the soil. Turn the soil over so all organic matter is covered completely.

Because melons require well-drained soils, work the soil into ridges or hills 4 to 8 inches high and 12 to 14 inches wide for planting. Heavier soils require higher ridges. Place the rows of muskmelons and honeydews 6 to 8 feet apart, and watermelons 10 to 12 feet apart.

Plant

Melons are warm-season crops and easily injured by frost. Do not plant the seeds until the soil warms in the spring and all danger of frost has passed.

Black plastic mulch can warm the soil, giving the melons an earlier start on growth.

Plant the seeds in hills in groups of six to eight seeds at 1 to 1½ inches deep. Planting several seeds per spot helps the seedlings push through. Place the hills 2 to 3 feet apart.

Fine sandy soils or heavy clay soils often crust when dry, so if the weather is dry after planting, moisten the hill to soften the soil.

You can harvest 10 to 12 days earlier if you use transplants. Plant seeds in peat pots 2 to 4 weeks before transplanting them into the garden before the second true leaf opens.

Fertilize

Melons do best with small amounts of fertilizer in two or three applications. Apply it in a band along the row.

Cover the fertilizer and plant the seeds so that they do not touch the fertilizer.

Before the runners on the vines are about 6 inches long, scatter 2 to 3 pounds of fertilizer per 60 to 90 feet of row 2 to 3 feet to the side of the row and mix it lightly with the soil.

For **watermelons**, apply a fertilizer high in phosphorus, such as 10-10-10, at a rate of 4 pounds per 1,000 square feet (60 to 90 feet of row). Make a trench on the planting bed 4 to 6 inches deep and 2 inches from the side of the row. Cover the fertilizer and plant so the seeds do not touch the fertilizer.

Before the runners on the vines are about 6 inches long, scatter 2 to 3 pounds of fertilizer per 60 to 90 feet of row 2 to 3 feet to the side of the row and mix it lightly with the soil.

Fertilize **cantaloupes** and **honeydews** with 2 to 3 pounds of fertilizer for every 60 to 70 feet of row. Phosphorus, the second number on the fertilizer label, is most important for cantaloupes at planting, and nitrogen is important when the vines begin to run.

Make the second fertilizer application to the side of the row when vines begin to run.

Water

Keep the soil consistently moist but not soaked throughout the season.

The male watermelon flower (left) begins appearing first, and the females start blooming a week or two after. Female flowers have a small swelling or fruit at the base of the flower; males do not.

Care

Melon plants break through the soil 10 to 12 days after planting. After the plants are up, thin them to three to four plants per hill.

After the plants have two or three leaves, thin them again, leaving two plants per hill. Insect or other damage often makes another thinning unnecessary.

Keep weeds away from the plants, especially at the beginning of the season while the plants are getting started. When hoeing, be careful not to cut too deeply into the soil near the melon plants, or you will damage the roots.

Melon plants have separate male and female flowers on each plant, and bees cross-pollinate the flowers. Poor pollination causes the female flowers to fall off the vines or the fruits to be poorly shaped, which is a common problem with watermelon.

Increase fruit size by pruning watermelons to two fruits per plant for large varieties or four to six fruits per plant on small varieties. Pruning also increases the size of cantaloupe fruits, but it usually is not needed.

Source: Bruno Girin (CC BY-SA 2.0)

Cantaloupe

Diseases

Rotating crops is vital for disease control. To prevent the buildup of diseases, do not plant melons in the same place more than once every 3 or 4 years. If spots do appear on the leaves and no insects are present, you may need to apply a fungicide.

Common diseases of melons in Texas are Alternaria leaf spot, anthracnose, blossom end rot, damping-off, downy mildew, Fusarium wilt, powdery mildew, southern blight (also called fruit and stem rot, southern wilt, southern stem rot), squash leaf curl, sunburn, and yellow vine.

For more information, descriptions, control recommendations, and photos of common vegetable diseases, see the "Dis-eases" section starting on page 40.

Before using a pesticide, read the label and always follow cautions, warnings, and directions.

Insects

The most common insect pests are aphids, cabbage loopers, cucumber beetles, flea beetles, leafminers, spider mites, and spotted cucumber beetles.

Photographs, descriptions, and control recommendations for common insect pests are in the "Insects and other pests" section starting on page 61.

Harvest

Most melons require 80 to 100 days from planting to harvest.

Cantaloupes: Harvest when the fruit rind changes to yellowish orange, the stem begins to separate or slip from the fruit, and the fragrance becomes strong. The outer rind should not have any green color.

If left long enough, the stem will naturally separate from the fruit. This is called "full slip." Use fruit at this stage within 36 to 48 hours, as it will spoil soon.

For better quality, harvest

Source: humboldthead (CC BY 2.0)

Store cut watermelon in the refrigerator.

them at the "half slip" stage, when the stem is partially separated from the fruit.

Cantaloupes can improve in flavor after harvest because the flesh mellows.

Honeydews: Harvest when the skin begins to turn yellow and the end of the fruit opposite the stem (blossom end) begins to soften.

Do not harvest honeydew melons too early because the sugar content does not increase after harvest.

Watermelons: Judging the ripeness of watermelons requires skill and experience. Some signs of ripeness in watermelons are:

- *Death or drying of the tendril:* The tendril near the point where the melon is attached to the vine dries when ripe. This is the most dependable sign.
- *Dull sound when thumped:* This varies with the gardener and the size and type of melon and often is inaccurate.
- *Change in color of rind:* Ripe melons often lose their glossy color.
- *Change in color of the soil spot:* The spot where the melon rests on the soil takes on a creamy, streaked color.

Use a knife to cut watermelons from the vine.

Store

If possible, refrigerate melons for 5 to 15 days. You can store uncut watermelons at room temperature for about a week.

Refrigerate cut melons for no more than 5 days.

Cleanup

To reduce the potential for insect and disease problems next year, remove all the plant material and smooth the bed.

Okra

Best varieties for Texas

- **Annie Oakley** (compact)
- **Blondy** (compact)
- **Burgundy**
- **Cajun Delight**
- **Clemson Spineless**
- **Emerald**
- **Lee**
- **Louisiana Green**
- **Stewart's Zee Best** (heirloom)
- **Velvet**

Choose the site

For good yields, grow okra in full sunlight in fertile, well-drained soil.

Prep the soil

Remove all rocks and trash from the soil. Spade or turn the soil as deeply as possible. Okra grows best in soil that has been worked 8 to 10 inches deep. Then rake the soil smooth.

Work the soil only when it is dry enough to not stick to garden tools.

Plant

For the best yields, plant okra in the spring 2 to 3 weeks after all danger of frost has passed. In the fall, plant at least 3 months before the first fall frost.

Plant the okra seeds about 1 inch deep and 2 inches apart in the row. Space the rows at least 3 feet apart.

Once the okra is up and growing, thin out the plants to about 1 foot apart.

Fertilize

Before planting, use 2 to 3 pounds of fertilizer such as 10-10-10 or 15-5-10 for each 100 square feet of garden. Spread it evenly over the area, and then mix it well into the top 3 to 4 inches of soil.

Source: lhooq38 (CC BY-ND 2.0)

Okra pods

Water

Okra does fairly well in dry weather. However, if you water the plants every 7 to 10 days, the yield will be higher. Sandy soils will need water more often than clay soils.

Care

Cultivate around the okra plants to remove weeds and grass. To avoid damaging the okra roots, pull the weeds that are close to the plants by hand.

After the first harvest, apply 1 cup of garden fertilizer for each 10 feet of row, scattering it evenly between the rows. Mix it lightly with the soil. Water the plants after fertilizing.

Diseases

Diseases on okra are most severe in cloudy, damp weather. Check the plants daily and if diseases appear, treat them with an approved fungicide such as neem oil or sulfur.

Common diseases of okra in Texas are Fusarium wilt, leaf spot, root knot nematodes, southern blight, and yellow leaf mosaic.

For more information, descriptions, control recommendations, and photos of common vegetable diseases, see the "Diseases" section starting on page 40. Before using a pesticide, read the label and always follow cautions, warnings, and directions.

Insects

The most common insect pests are aphids, banded cucumber beetles, and stink bugs.

Photographs, descriptions, and control recommendations for common vegetable insect pests are in the "Insects and other pests" section starting on page 61.

Source: Bob Richmond (CC BY 2.0)   Source: Paul and Jill (CC BY 2.0)

Okra pods appear 3 or 4 days after the plant blooms.   **Chill okra right after harvesting.**

Harvest

Okra plants produce large flowers about 2 months after planting, and the pods will be ready to pick 3 to 4 days later.

Harvest them when they are 3 to 4 inches long. If the okra gets too large, it will be tough and stringy. Pick the okra every 1 to 2 days, or yields will decrease.

You can easily save okra seeds for next season by leaving some of the last pods on the plant until they get very large.

Remove them and allow them to dry. The seeds will shell easily from the pods.

Store

Chill the pods immediately after harvest. Store okra for no more than 3 to 5 days in the refrigerator.

Cleanup

Clean the bed of all plant material, and put the okra leaves and stems in a compost pile.

Onions

Best varieties for Texas

Onions are categorized by day length. "Short-day" onions start making bulbs early in the year when the days are 10 to 12 hours long. They don't store well because they have a high water concentration.

Intermediate-day onions are best for North and West Texas; short-day onions are best for East, Central, and South Texas.

Short day (11 to 12 hours)

- **Red**
  Red Bone
  Rio Santiago
  Sakata Red
  Red Burgandy
- **White**
  Cirrus
  Marquesa
  TX Early White
  Crystal Wax
- **Yellow**
  Chula Vista
  Cougar
  Jaguar
  Legend
  Linda Vista
  Mercedes
  Prowler
  Safari
  Sweet Sunrise
  TX 1015Y
  Early Grano 502
  Granex

Intermediate day (12 to 13 hours)

- **Red**
  Fuego
- **White**
  Alabaster
  Mid Star
  Sierra Blanca
  Spano
- **Yellow**
  Caballero
  Cimarron
  Riviera
  Utopia
  Yula

Source: sproutsprout67 (CC BY 2.0)

Planting onion sets

Choose the site

Onions grow best in full sunlight and well-drained soils.

Prep the soil

Remove all rocks and trash from the soil. Work the soil 8 to 10 inches deep. Then break up the remaining clods and rake the soil smooth.

Work the garden soil only when it is dry enough not to stick to garden tools.

Plant

Onions can stand temperatures well below freezing. You may plant them using seeds, small bulbs called sets, or transplants.

Seeding costs the least but takes longer before the onions are ready. When seeding onions for bulbs, plant them ¼ inch deep during October through December.

Place the seeds 1 inch apart. When the plants are about 6 inches tall, thin them to one plant every 2 to 3 inches. You may eat the extra plants as green onions. Plant sets or transplants ¾ inch deep and 3 inches apart. Do not transplant onions more than 1 inch deep.

Fertilize

Onions grow best when the garden soil is fertilized correctly. Spread 2 to 3 pounds of a fertilizer such as 10-10-10 over 100-square-feet of garden area. Measure and spread the fertilizer, and mix it into the top 3 to 4 inches of soil.

Water

Watering once a week usually is enough in the spring. But you may need to water more often during dry, windy weather. Water the onions slowly and deeply to help grow strong, healthy roots.

Care

Weeds are easy to pull or cut when they are 3 to 4 inches tall. Do not let weeds or grasses grow large because they compete with onions for nutrients.

If you use a hoe to remove weeds and grass, do not chop too deeply, or you may cut the onion roots. Pull all weeds by hand when possible.

When the onion plants have 5 to 6 leaves, apply fertilizer again to help the plants and bulbs grow larger. Each leaf forms a ring in the bulb—a plant with more leaves has more rings and larger bulbs.

Use about ½ cup of fertilizer for each 10 feet of onion row, scattering the fertilizer evenly between the rows.

Water the onions after adding the fertilizer.

Diseases

Onion diseases can cause brown leaf tips or brown spots on the middle and lower parts of the leaves. Common diseases of onions in Texas are downy mildew, iris yellow spot, pow-dery mildew, purple blotch, and root knot nematodes.

Treatment options include neem oil, sulfur, and other fungicides.

For more information, descriptions, control recommendations, and photos of common vegetable diseases, see the "Diseases" section starting on page 40. Before using a pesticide, read the label and always follow cautions, warnings, and directions.

Insects

The most common insect pests are aphids, banded cucumber beetles, beet armyworms, root maggots, and thrips.

Photographs, descriptions, and control recommendations for common vegetable insect pests are in the "Insects and other pests" section starting on page 61.

Harvest

Onions seeded in October/December or transplanted in January/February should produce bulbs in May/July. If used as green onions, pick them from the time they are pencil size until they begin to form bulbs.

Source: MissMessie (CC BY-SA 2.0)

Harvest bulb onions when the tops begin to fall over.

For dry-bulb onions, let the plants grow larger. Harvest them when the onions are 2 to 4 inches in diameter. They are ready when the main stem begins to get weak and fall over.

Pull the plants out of the soil and leave them lying in the garden for 1 to 2 days to dry. Then remove the tops and roots and let them keep drying in baskets or boxes.

Store

Refrigerate the bulbs or store them in a dry, airy place such as in a wire net in the garage or carport. Keep them cool, dry, and separated. If you wrap the onions separately in foil and refrigerate them, they can keep up to a year.

Refrigerate green onions for up to a week after harvest.

Cleanup

To reduce the potential for insect and disease problems next year, remove all the plant material and smooth the bed.

Peas

Best varieties for Texas

Southern peas are warm-season crops:

- **Southern**
    - Blackeye #5
    - Champion Cream
    - Colossus
    - Crowder
    - Mississippi Silver
    - Pink Eye Purple Hull
    - Texas Cream 8
    - Texas Pinkeye
    - Zipper Cream

Amish Snap, snap, and sugar snap peas are cool-season crops in Texas:

- **Sugar snap**
    - Cascadia (60 days from planting to maturity)
    - Premium (51 days)
    - Sugar Ann (60 days)
    - Sugar Bob (55 days)
    - Super Sugar Snap (65 days)

Blackeyed peas

- **Heirloom**
    - Amish Snap (60 days)
- **Snow**
    - Dwarf White Sugar
    - Mammoth Melting Sugar
    - Oregon Giant
    - Oregon Sugar Pod
    - Oregon Sugar Pod II
    - Short N' Sweet

Choose the site

Peas grow well in a variety of soil types if the area drains well. They prefer fine sandy

Insects

The most common insect pests are aphids, armyworms, cucumber beetles, cutworms, leafminers, loopers, and stink bugs.

Source: saiberiac (CC BY 2.0)

Source: Doug Beckers (CC BY-SA 2.0)

Harvest sugar snap peas about 5 to 7 days after blooming.

Photographs, descriptions, and control recommendations for common vegetable insect pests are in the "Insects and other pests" section starting on page 61.

Harvest

Warm-season peas are ready to harvest about 55 to 80 days after you sow the seeds. Pick them when the pods are filled well, and their color has changed from green to purple, silver, or straw, depending on the type of pea.

Harvest **cool-season peas** when the individual peas have grown to the size of BBs, or when the pods have reached their full length, usually 5 to 7 days after flowering.

Pick the peas at least every other day to ensure that the pods are sweet and free of fibers. If you find an overgrown pod that you missed earlier, remove it to keep the plant blooming and producing longer.

Store

Because the quality of **southern peas** deteriorates quickly after harvest, they are best if shelled and eaten the same day they are picked. If they must be stored, refrigerate unshelled peas for 3 or 4 days. Store fresh-shelled peas in plastic bags for 5 to 7 days at 32°F.

Refrigerate sugar snap and snow pea pods in a plastic bag for up to 2 weeks. Unlike fresh green peas, the quality of the stored pods deteriorates only slightly.

Cleanup

To reduce the potential for insect and disease problems next year, remove all the plant material and smooth the bed.

Peppers

Best varieties for Texas

- **Hot peppers**
  Hidalgo Serrano
  Hungarian Wax
  Jalapeño
  Long Red Cayenne
  TAM Mild Jalapeño

- **Sweet peppers**
  Bell Tower
  Big Bertha
  California Wonder
  Gypsy
  Jupiter
  Yolo Wonder

Choose the site

Peppers grow in all types of soils but do best in heavier, well-drained soils. Plant them in areas that receive at least 6 hours of sunlight each day.

Prep the soil

Several weeks before planting, work the soil 8 to 10 inches deep and rake it several times to break up the large clods. Work the soil only when it is dry enough not to stick to garden tools.

Incorporate large amounts of organic matter—such as compost, peat moss or rotted hay—into the soil, especially if you are working with heavy clay.

Plant

Because a few plants will feed most families, it is best to buy pepper plants rather than grow them from seed. Buy healthy plants that are 4 to 6

Source: 4nitsirk (CC BY-SA 2.0)
Bell peppers

Source: OakleyOriginals (CC BY 2.0)　　　　Source: H. Zell (GFDL or CC BY-SA 3.0)

For a family of four, eight to ten sweet bell pepper plants (left) and three to four hot cayenne pepper plants are usually sufficient.

inches tall. About three to four hot pepper plants and eight to 10 sweet pepper plants usually are enough for a family of four.

Peppers grow best in warm weather. For the spring crop, plant them only when all danger of cold weather has passed. Plant fall peppers 12 to 16 weeks before the first expected frost.

Dig the transplant holes 3 to 4 inches deep and about 1½ feet apart. Space the rows at least 3 feet apart. Before planting the peppers, fill the holes with water and let it soak in.

It is best to transplant peppers in the evening or on a cloudy day. This keeps the plants from drying too much and wilting.

Move the plants carefully and set them in the transplant holes. Fill the hole with soil and tamp it down lightly around the plant. Do not cover the roots deeper than the original soil ball.

Around each plant, leave a slightly sunken area to hold water. Water the plants after planting.

Fertilize

Place about 2 level tablespoons of fertilizer such as 10-10-10 on the soil in the planting area. Mix it well with the soil.

Water

Water the plants enough to keep them from wilting. Slow,

deep watering helps the root system grow strong.

Do not let the plants wilt because this reduces the yield and quality of the peppers.

Care

Hoe or till the soil lightly. Deep tilling cuts the pepper roots and slows growth. Pull by hand any weeds that are close to the plants.

After the first pepper begins to enlarge, place about 2 tablespoons of fertilizer around each plant about 6 inches from the stem. Water the plant after adding the fertilizer to increase the peppers' yield and quality.

Diseases

Because diseases can be a problem on peppers, watch the plants closely. In mild weather, diseases start easily.

The most common diseases of peppers in Texas are bacterial leaf spot, damping-off, leaf spot, mosaic, Phytophthora blight, powdery mildew, southern blight, and sunscald.

For more information, descriptions, control recommendations, and photos of common vegetable diseases, see the "Diseases" section starting on page 40. Before using a pesticide, read the label and always follow cautions, warnings, and directions.

Insects

The most common insect pests are aphids, beet armyworms, cabbage loopers, corn earworms, cutworms, flea beetles, and stink bugs.

Photographs, descriptions, and control recommendations for common vegetable insect pests are in the "Insects and other pests" section starting on page 61.

Harvest

If you pick the peppers as they mature, the yields will be greater. The first peppers should be ready 8 to 10 weeks after transplanting.

Pick bell peppers when they become shiny, firm, and dark

Source: OakleyOriginals (CC BY 2.0)

Harvest peppers as they mature for a more abundant crop.

Red jalapeños are not necessarily hotter than green ones.

green. Harvest when they are 4 to 5 inches long and have full, well-formed lobes; immature peppers are pale, soft, pliable, and thin fleshed.

If left on the plant, most peppers will turn red and are still good to eat.

Harvest most hot peppers when they are 2 to 2½ inches long and turn red or yellow, depending on the variety.

Jalapeños are mature when they reach a good size and develop a deep, dark green sheen; mature peppers turn orange or red, but this does not mean that they are hotter.

Store

Store peppers in the vegetable crisper of the refrigerator. Use them within 3 to 5 days after harvest.

Cleanup

To reduce the potential for insect and disease problems next year, remove all the plant material and smooth the bed.

Potatoes

Best varieties for Texas

- **Red flesh**
  Dark Red Norland
  Norland
  Red LaSoda
  Viking

- **White flesh**
  Atlantic
  Gemchip
  Kennebec
  Superior

- **Yellow flesh**
  Yukon Gold

- **Russet**
  Century Russet
  Norgold M
  Russet Norkatah

Choose the site

For best production, potatoes need full sun. They do best in a loose, well-drained, slightly acid soil.

Poorly drained soils often cause poor stands and a small harvest. Heavy soils—those with a high clay content—can cause the tubers to be small and rough.

Prep the soil

Remove the rocks, trash, and large sticks from the soil. Spade the soil 8 to 12 inches deep, turning the earth over to cover all plant material.

Work the soil into beds 10 to 12 inches high and 36 inches apart. Bedding is vital for drainage.

Because potatoes need adequate fertilizer early in the season, apply most of the fertilizer just before planting. Use 2 to 3 pounds of complete fertilizer such as 10-20-10 for each 30 feet of row in bands 2 inches to each

Source: woodleywonderworks (CC BY 2.0)

Planting potato seed pieces in trenches

Prep the seed potatoes

Unlike most other vege-tables, Irish potatoes are not grown from seed. Instead, pieces from the potato itself start new plants.

Buy good seed potatoes that are free of disease and chemi-cals. Do not buy potatoes from a grocery store for planting.

The seed potato contains buds or "eyes" that sprout and grow into plants. The seed piece provides food for the plant until it develops a root system. If the seed is too small, it will produce a weak plant.

One pound of seed potatoes will make 9 to 10 seed pieces.

For a spring crop, cut large seed potatoes into pieces weigh-ing about 1½ to 2 ounces, about

side and 1 inch below the seed piece. Do not allow the fertilizer to touch the seed piece.

To apply the fertilizer, flat-ten the beds at 6 to 8 inches high and 10 to 12 inches wide. Using the corner of a hoe or stick, open a trench about 4 inches deep on each side of the bed.

Apply half of the fertilizer—about 2 cups for each 30 feet of row—in each trench. Plant the seed pieces in the row between the two bands of fertilizer.

Source: Mathias Karlsson (GDFL, CC-BY-SA-3.0, or CC BY-SA 2.5-2.0-1.0)

A seed potato with sprouts. Each seed piece should have at least one good eye.

Potato plant

Source: Scott Bauer, USDA ARS

Many colors and varieties of potatoes are available.

the size of a medium chicken egg. Each seed piece must have at least one good eye.

Cut the seeds 5 or 6 days before planting and keep the cut seed in a well-ventilated spot so it can heal over to prevent rotting when planted in cold, wet, or very hot weather. Plants killed by a late spring frost will not come back if the seed piece is rotten.

Treating the seed pieces with a fungicide before planting helps prevent diseases.

For fall-grown potatoes, plant small, uncut potatoes because they are more resistant to rotting in hot weather than are cut potatoes. Select mature potatoes about 1½ inches in diameter.

Potatoes have a rest period that must be broken before they will sprout. The rest period is more easily broken in small, mature potatoes.

To be sure the rest period is broken, store small seed potatoes under warm, damp conditions for 2 weeks before planting by placing them in a shady spot and covering them with moist burlap bags or mulch. The potatoes should have small sprouts at planting time.

Because the seed is usually more available in the spring than in the fall, many gardeners buy extra seed in the spring and hold it over for fall planting.

For best storage, keep the seed potatoes in a cool, humid spot, such as the bottom of a refrigerator.

Do not save your potato seeds for more than 1 year. This can cause virus diseases to build up and reduce yield.

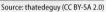
Source: thatedeguy (CC BY-SA 2.0)

Source: Jolly Janner

Starting a potato bag, left. Growing potatoes in a tall bag minimizes the amount of digging needed at harvest. As potato plants grow (right), unfold the bag enough to add about 4 more inches of soil.

Plant

Plant potatoes when the soil temperature 4 inches deep reaches about 50°F, or about 3 weeks before the last spring frost. In most areas of Texas, plant potatoes in February or early March. If the potatoes are planted too early, the tops can be frozen off by spring frost.

For a fall crop, plant about 110 days before the first expected frost, or mid-August in most areas.

Use a hoe or stick to open a trench about 3 inches deep down the center of the bed. Drop the seed pieces 10 to 12 inches apart in the trench.

Step on each seed piece after dropping it to ensure good contact with the soil.

Cover the seed about 3 inches deep. If covered too deeply, the plants will be slow to break through the soil and more subject to disease and seed decay.

If you are planting potatoes in a tall bag, roll or fold down the top edge of the bag, add soil to about 4 inches deep, and place the seed potatoes, spaced evenly at least 6 inches apart, on the surface. Then cover them with about 3 inches of soil.

When the plants grow to about 8 inches tall, unfold the bag some and add about 4 inches more soil. Repeat this process until the bag is full.

Fertilize

The plant must have adequate moisture and fertilizer

when the tubers are forming. This usually occurs when the plants are 6 to 8 inches tall.

Apply 1 cup of fertilizer for each 30 feet of row beside the plants when they are about 4 inches tall.

Water

During growth, keep the soil moisture supply constant. Water the fertilizer into the soil, especially on sandy soils.

Moisture stress followed by irrigation or rainfall can cause growth cracks and second growth. Hot weather accompanying rainfall can break the rest period of developing tubers and cause them to sprout in the soil.

Too much water enlarges the pores on the tubers and makes them rot easily in storage.

Source: Keith Weller

Potato plants usually produce flowers and sometimes produce fruits.

Care

All tubers produced on a potato plant arise from above the seed piece. Because the seed piece is planted only 3 inches deep, pull soil toward the plant as it grows. This gives the tubers a place to form.

Some gardeners use thick mulch for this purpose. Potatoes formed in soft mulch often are smoother and have a better shape than those grown in soil, especially if the soil is heavy.

As the potatoes enlarge, protect them from sunlight, or they will turn green. Apply a thick layer of mulch when the plants are 8 to 10 inches tall to block sunlight, reduce soil temperature, and increase yield and quality.

Potato plants usually produce flowers and sometimes produce fruits. The fruits bear the true seed of the potato plant. They look like small tomatoes but cannot be eaten.

Diseases

Common diseases of potatoes in Texas are black leg, early blight, Fusarium wilt, late blight, mosaic, Verticillium wilt, root knot nematodes, and southern blight.

Check the plants daily and treat them with an approved fungicide if diseases appear. Neem oil, sulfur, and other fungicides are available.

A good rotation program is an effective way to control most potato diseases. If possible, do not plant potatoes in the same place more than once every 3 years. Do not follow or precede potatoes with eggplant, okra, peppers, or tomatoes. Seed piece treatment is especially important if your garden is too small for adequate rotation.

For more information, descriptions, control recommendations, and photos of common vegetable diseases, see the "Diseases" section starting on page 40. Before using a pesticide, read the label and always follow cautions, warnings, and directions.

Insects

The most common insect pests are aphids, banded cucumber beetles, beet armyworms, flea beetles, cabbage loopers, Colorado potato beetles, cutworms, flea beetles, leafhoppers, leafminers, and wireworms.

Photographs, descriptions,

After harvesting potatoes, remove any adhering soil, allow them to dry, and store them unwashed.

and control recommendations for common vegetable insect pests are in the "Insects and other pests" section starting on page 61.

Harvest

Most potato varieties are ready to dig 95 to 110 days after planting. Potatoes are ready to harvest when the tops begin to die and the potato skin becomes firm. The skin is set when it does not scrape easily when rubbed with the thumb. Speed skin set by cutting back the tops of the plants.

Most of the potatoes should weigh 6 to 12 ounces at harvest. You can harvest small "new potatoes" during the growing season by carefully digging beside the plants with your fingers.

To harvest potatoes, dig under the plants with a shovel or spading fork. Keep the fork 8 to 10 inches away from the plant to avoid cutting the potatoes.

Raise the plants and remove any adhering soil. Dig potatoes when the soil is moist. If it is too wet, the soil will stick to the potatoes; if too dry, dirt clods will bruise the potatoes.

Pull the potatoes from the vines and handle them carefully to prevent damage; damaged potatoes do not store well.

Store

Allow the potatoes to dry; then store them unwashed in a cool, dry, dark area with plenty of air movement.

Cleanup

After digging the potatoes, place the tops in the compost pile. The spring potato crop often can be followed with a summer crop such as southern peas.

Pumpkins

Best varieties for Texas

- **Small**
  - Baby Bear
  - Jack Be Little
  - Munchkin
  - Mystic
  - Small Sugar
  - Triple Treat
- **Medium**
  - Bumpkin
  - Howden
  - Jack O'-Lantern
- **Large**
  - Aladdin
  - Big Max
  - Connecticut Field
  - Fairytale
  - Magic Lantern
  - Merlin
  - Prizewinner

Note: In Texas, the weather is too hot for the large pumpkin varieties to turn orange by Halloween. You can still carve them for jack o'lanterns, but you will have to pick them while they're still green.

Choose the site

Pumpkins prefer well-drained, sandy loam soils with a pH range of 6.5 to 7.5; avoid soils with a high clay content. They need full sun.

Prep the soil

Remove rocks, large sticks, and trash. To enrich the soil,

Pumpkin plants need to be grown in full sun.

The orange Baby Bear pumpkins, and the white Baby Boo pumpkins

Source: VasenkaPhotography (CC BY 2.0)

turn under the small pieces of plant material.

Spade the soil to 8 to 12 inches deep. Spread 2 to 3 inches of organic material such as compost, leaves, or rotted hay over the planting area. Then till to mix this organic material into the top 8 to 10 inches of soil.

If you are planting a large pumpkin variety, create rows that are 10 to 12 feet apart; for medium varieties, space the rows 7 to 9 feet apart; and for miniature varieties, 6 to 8 feet apart.

Plant

Pumpkins are sensitive to cold. Plant them in the spring after all danger of frost has passed.

Plant two or three seeds about 1 inch deep in each hole. For the large pumpkin varieties, space the plantings 5 to 6 feet apart in the rows; for medium varieties, space them 3 to 4 feet apart; and for miniature varieties, 2 feet apart. Water after planting the seeds.

When the young plants are well established, thin each group to the best plant per hill. Add mulch to keep the fruit from touching the soil and being more susceptible to diseases.

Fertilize

Before planting, add 2 to 3 tablespoons of fertilizer such as 10-10-10 for each hill. Scatter the fertilizer evenly over a

A pumpkin just starting

Munchkin—less than 3 inches wide

2-foot-square area. Work it into the top 3 to 4 inches of soil.

Three weeks after the plants start blooming, side-dress with ¼ pound of 10-10-10 per 10 feet of row.

Water

Pumpkins have shallow roots, so keep the soil uniformly moist. Water deeply and regularly, especially while they are blooming and setting fruit.

If the weather is very dry, water the squash at least once a week. Sandy soils need to be watered more often than do heavy clay soils.

Care

Remove all weeds, being careful not to damage the roots of the pumpkin plants.

Diseases

Common diseases of pumpkins in Texas are Alternaria leaf spot, anthracnose, downy mildew, fruit rot, gummy stem blight, and powdery mildew.

For more information, descriptions, control recommendations, and photos of common vegetable diseases, see the "Diseases" section starting on page 40. Before using a pesticide, read the label and always follow cautions, warnings, and directions.

Insects and other pests

The most common pumpkin pests are aphids, leafminers, loopers, rootworms, spider mites, squash bugs, squash vine borers, and whiteflies.

Source: mRio (CC BY 2.0)

Fairytale pumpkins

Source: HalfGig (CC BY-SA 3.0)

Connecticut Field pumpkin

Photographs, descriptions, and control recommendations for common vegetable insect pests are in the "Insects and other pests" section starting on page 61.

a deep, solid color (usually orange).

Use a sharp knife or pruning shears to cut them from the vines. Leaving a long neck on the fruit is desirable.

Harvest

Harvest pumpkins when the skin is hard and has turned

Store

Store pumpkins in a dry area at 50°F to 55°F. Under these conditions, they will keep for 2 to 3 months.

Source: ancapron (CC BY 2.0)

Small Sugar pumpkin

Cleanup

To avoid disease buildup in the soil, do not plant pumpkins, cucumbers, or squash in the same place within 3 to 5 years.

Compost old pumpkin vines or work them into the soil well before the spring planting season.

Radishes

Best varieties for Texas

- **Red**
  Champion
  Cherry Belle
  Early Scarlet
  Early Scarlet Globe

- **White**
  Chinese White Winter
  Summer Cross
  White Icicle

Choose the site

Radishes can grow in partial shade. They require very little room and mature quickly. They are well suited to small gardens, flower beds, and containers.

Prep the soil

Radishes need loose, well-drained soil to allow the roots to expand easily. If the soil is crusty, the roots become mis-shapen.

Remove rocks, trash, and large sticks from the planting area. Mix small pieces of plant material such as grass and leaves into the soil to make it richer.

Spade the soil to a depth of 8 to 12 inches. Turn each shovelful completely over so all the plant material is covered.

Scatter 1 cup of fertilizer, such as 10-20-10, on the soil for each 10 feet of row to be planted. Rake the soil until it is smooth and work up the beds as shown.

Source: OakleyOriginals (CC BY 2.0)
Radish seedlings

Source: anathea (CC BY 2.0)
Young radishes

Plant

Plant the seeds as soon as you can work the soil in the spring. Using a hoe handle, stick, or similar object, make a furrow ½ inch deep down the center of the ridge.

Plant the seeds ½ inch deep and 1 inch apart in the row. Cover them lightly with loose soil and sprinkle them with water.

The plants should be up in 4 to 6 days. Make several plantings 8 to 10 days apart for a steady supply of

radishes. They will be ready for harvest about 4 to 5 weeks from planting.

Fertilize

After the plants sprout, apply ¼ cup of a nitrogen-based fertilizer (21-0-0) per 10 feet of row. Scatter it beside the plants; this is called side-dressing. Water the fertilizer into the soil.

Water

Water the plants well each week if it does not rain.

Care

Scratch the soil around the plant slightly with a rake or hand tool to keep the soil from crusting.

Begin thinning the radishes when the roots start expanding.

Source: OakleyOriginals (CC BY 2.0)
Radishes can be harvested 4 to 5 weeks after planting.

Harvest radishes when they are young and tender.

Pull every other plant. You can eat the larger roots; those left in the row will continue to grow without being crowded.

Keep the radishes free of weeds, which rob weak root systems of nutrients and moisture.

Diseases

Because radishes mature so quickly, diseases are usually not a problem. Check the plants daily and treat them with an approved fungicide if diseases appear.

Common diseases of radishes in Texas are bacterial leaf spot, powdery mildew, and white rust.

For more information, descriptions, control recommendations, and photos of common vegetable diseases, see the "Diseases" section starting on page 40. Before using a pesticide, read the label and always follow cautions, warnings, and directions.

Insects

The most common insect pests are beet armyworms, flea beetles, cabbage loopers, grasshoppers, harlequin bugs, and root maggots.

A daikon radish is also known as a white radish, winter radish, Oriental radish, and long white radish.

Photographs, descriptions, and control recommendations for common vegetable insect pests are in the "Insects and other pests" section starting on page 61.

Harvest

Harvest radishes when they are young, tender, and about 1 inch in diameter. If left in the ground too long, they get tough and stringy.

To harvest, pull the radishes, cut off the tops and small roots, and put those in a compost pile.

Store

Wash the radishes well and place them in plastic bags in the refrigerator. They will keep 2 to 3 weeks or until the next planting is ready for harvest.

Cleanup

After the radishes get too old or start going to seed, pull and place them in a compost pile if the soil is to be replanted soon.

If the soil is to be left idle, spade the old radishes and tops into the soil to help enrich it.

Sweet potatoes

Best varieties for Texas

- **Beauregard/Centennial**
- **Jewel**
- **Vardaman**

Choose the site

Sweet potatoes require full sun and a warm climate. Plant them in a well-drained, fine sandy loam soil with a slightly acidic pH 5 to 7.5. This allows the sweet potato to grow easily but not remain in a moist environment that encourages rot and disease.

Prep the soil

Have the soil tested before planting. It may need only nitrogen. Most areas of Texas have enough phosphorus and potassium in the soil, except for the eastern counties with sandy soils and 40 to 60 inches of rainfall per year; these areas may lack potassium.

Incorporate compost or a complete fertilizer into the soil.

Work the soil into beds 8 inches high and 3 to 4 feet apart to ensure that it drains well and warms quickly in early spring.

Prep the slips

Unlike other vegetables, sweet potatoes are propagated from slips, also called vine cuttings. You can produce slips at home, buy them at a local garden store, or order them online.

To produce slips, buy healthy, disease-free sweet potatoes from a local market.

Source: anathea (CC BY 2.0)
Sweet potato slip just beginning

Source for all: jessicareeder(CC BY 2.0)

Plant sweet potato slips after shoots have formed and when the soil temperature stays above 55°F.

Scrub them clean and then cut them in half. Suspend each half over a jar of water by inserting toothpicks so that half is submerged in the water. Place the sweet potato near a window for warmth and sunlight. Over the next few weeks, shoots will form on top.

Plant

Wait 2 weeks after the last frost to begin planting them outside. The optimal planting time is when the soil temperature at planting depth is over 65°F in the spring and at least 150 days before anticipated 55°F soil temperature in the fall.

Sweet potatoes can also tolerate light frosts as long as the soil temperature stays above 55°F.

Fertilize

Have the soil tested to determine what nutrients to add. General recommendations for a 100-square-foot garden are 19 ounces of 13-13-13.

Water

Sweet potatoes need 10 to 20 inches of water per season. Because rain falls sporadically throughout the season, water them especially at first while the slip is getting established. Transplanted slips are extremely sensitive to water stress during the first month of establishment.

A row of sweet potatoes planted in a tall furrow for good drainage

To keep the tubers from rotting, do not water them in the last 2 to 3 weeks before harvest.

Care

Keep the beds weed-free until the vines have fully covered the bed. Maintaining a weed-free area, especially in the first 40 days after planting, improves yield quantity and quality at harvest.

Diseases

Common diseases of sweet potatoes in Texas are black rot, leaf spot, and root knot nematodes.

For more information, descriptions, control recommendations, and photos of common vegetable diseases, see the "Diseases" section starting on page 40. Before using a pesticide, read the label and always follow cautions, warnings, and directions.

Insects

The most common insect pests are banded cucumber beetles, beet armyworms, flea beetles, cabbage loopers, cutworms, and sweet potato weevils.

Photographs, descriptions, and control recommendations for common vegetable insect pests are in the "Insects and other pests" section starting on page 61.

Source Cuyahoga jco (CC BY 2.0)

Take care not to bruise the sweet potato's delicate skin at harvest.

Source: USDAgov (CC BY 2.0)

Sweet potatoes need to cure for at least 2 weeks in a warm, well-ventilated location.

Harvest

The sweet potato's delicate skin is easily bruised at harvest. Take care not to bruise the roots with a hoe, shovel, or other harvesting tool. Even dropping the potatoes into a bucket will injure the skin.

For home gardeners, the best time to harvest sweet potatoes is immediately before or just after the first fall frost. When the sweet potato leaves turn yellow, growth has stopped and the roots have matured. This is a good time for harvest.

Store

Cure the potatoes for at least 14 days in a warm, well-ventilated location. Store them in a cool, dry place.

Cleanup

To reduce the potential for insect and disease problems next year, remove all the plant material and smooth the bed.

Tomatillos

Best varieties for Texas

- Cape Gooseberry
- Golden Nugget
- Mayan Husk Tomato
- Mexican Husk
- Rendidora

Choose the site

Tomatillos prefer well-drained, sandy loam soils with a pH between 5.5 and 7.3. They do not do well in wet conditions. In general, they grow in any soil that is suitable for tomatoes.

Native to Mexico and Guatemala, tomatillos are sensitive to cold. The best growing conditions are 80°F to 90°F days with 60°F to 70°F nights, low humidity, and sparse rainfall.

Prep the soil

Remove large rocks, sticks, and other bits of trash from the planting area. Have your soil tested and fertilize it according to the test results and recommendations.

Work the garden soil only when it is dry enough not to stick to the garden tools. Several weeks before planting, work the top 8 to 10 inches of soil. Rake the soil to break up large clods.

Add 2 to 3 pounds of fertilizer such as 10-10-10 for every 100 square feet of garden area. Spread the fertilizer evenly over the area, and then mix it into the top 3 to 4 inches of soil.

Tomatillos grow best in soils that have lots of organic matter.

Source: Scarygami (CC BY-SA 2.0)
Tomatillo flowers and leaves

190

Tomatillo plants prefer soil that is organically rich.

If possible, spread 2 to 3 inches of organic material such as compost, leaves, or rotted hay over the planting area. Mix it into the top 4 to 6 inches of soil.

Plant

Tomatillos are normally planted as seed. You can also use cuttings since they root very easily.

Space Rendidora tomatillos 16 inches between the plants and 4 feet between the rows.

For other varieties, plant every 2 feet in rows 5 feet apart. If you are starting with seeds, plant 3 or 4 tomatillo seeds in each hill, with the hills 2 feet apart. When the plants reach 4 to 5 inches tall, thin them to one plant every 2 feet.

Fertilize

Add 1 to 2 level tablespoons of fertilizer every 3 to 4 weeks. Scatter it about 6 inches from the stalks, and then work it lightly into the soil. Water the plants after fertilizing.

Water

Water the tomatillo plants slowly and deeply to help them develop a strong root system. Do not let them wilt severely.

Care

Spread a 2- to 3-inch layer of organic material such as compost, leaves, or hay around the growing plants. Mulching helps stop weed growth and water loss from the soil.

You can let tomatillos grow on the ground or support them with stakes or cages. If you stake the tomatillos, put the stake in shortly after transplanting to lessen root damage.

To control weeds, pull them or hoe around the plants, but be careful to avoid damaging the tomatillo roots.

Diseases

Common diseases of tomatillos in Texas are black spot,

Source: regan76 (CC BY 2.0)

Pick tomatillos as soon as the papery husk bursts open.

powdery mildew, root knot nematodes, and tobacco mosaic virus.

For more information, descriptions, control recommendations, and photos of common vegetable diseases, see the "Diseases" section starting on page 40. Before using a pesticide, read the label and always follow warnings, and directions.

Insects

The most common insect pests are cutworms, tobacco budworms, and whiteflies.

Photos, descriptions, and control recommendations for these vegetable insect pests are in the "Insects and other pests" section starting on page 61.

Harvest

The plants begin bearing fruit 65 to 85 days after seeding or transplanting and continue for 1 to 2 months or until the first frost.

Pick the fruit just as the husk, or calyx, bursts. If left on the plant too long, the flavor and quality suffers. Then set out the fruit for 2 weeks to let the husks dry.

A plant may produce 60 to 200 fruits in a growing season. An average yield is 2½ pounds per plant.

Store

After the 2-week drying period, refrigerate tomatillos for up to 3 weeks.

Cleanup

To reduce the potential for insect and disease problems next year, remove all the plant material and smooth the bed.

Source: Gudlyf (CC BY 2.0)

Set out tomatillos for 2 weeks after harvest to allow the husks to dry.

Tomatoes

Best varieties for Texas

- **Small fruit**
  - Baxter's Early Bush
  - Cherry Grande
  - Juliet
  - Red Cherry
  - Small Fry
- **Large fruit**
  - Better Boy
  - Big Beef
  - Big Box
  - Bush Beefsteak
  - Carnival
  - Celebrity
  - Homestead

Choose the site

Tomatoes grow well in most of Texas if they are planted in soil that drains well. They need at least 6 hours of sunlight each day.

Prep the soil

Several weeks before planting, remove all rocks and trash from the soil and rake it to break up large clods.

Work the top 8 to 10 inches of soil. Work it only when it is dry enough not to stick to the garden tools.

Tomatoes grow best in soils that have lots of organic matter. If possible, spread 2 to 3 inches of organic material such as compost, leaves, or rotted hay over the planting area. Mix it into the top 4 to 6 inches of soil.

Add 2 to 3 pounds of fertilizer such as 10-10-10 for every 100 square feet of garden area. Spread the fertilizer evenly over the area; then mix it into the top 3 to 4 inches of soil.

Plant

Because most families need only a few tomato plants, it is

Buy tomato plants that are 6 to 8 inches tall.

usually best to use transplants and not grow tomatoes from seed. Buy healthy, green plants that are 6 to 8 inches tall.

In the spring, set out the plants after all danger of frost has passed. Transplant fall tomatoes in the garden about 100 days before the first expected frost.

If possible, set out the tomatoes on raised beds that are about 6 inches high. Make the transplant holes 3 to 4 inches deep and 2 to 4 feet apart in the row. For staked or caged plants, space the rows at least 3 feet apart. For unsupported plants, leave 4 to 5 feet between the rows.

Dig a hole 2 feet wide and 10 inches deep. Refill the hole with half soil and half organic matter. Mix 2 level tablespoons of fertilizer into the planting area.

Before placing transplants into the soil, fill the transplant holes with water and let it soak in.

Plant each transplant slightly deeper than it had been growing in its container. Pack the soil loosely around the plant. Leave a slightly sunken

Juliet cherry tomatoes

Yellow pear tomatoes

Big Beef tomatoes

Source: Mad Mod Smith (CC BY-SA 2.0)

Pruning tomato plants will produce a more orderly vine.

Source: Mark F. Levisay (CC BY 2.0)

Big Beef tomatoes, staked and tied with strips of cloth

area around each plant to hold water.

Transplant the tomatoes in the evening or on a cloudy day to keep them from drying too much and wilting.

Fertilize

When the first fruits are about 1 inch in diameter, scatter 1 level tablespoon of fertilizer around each plant. Scatter it about 6 inches from the stalks, and work it lightly into the soil.

Water the plants after fertilizing.

Fertilize the plants every 3 to 4 weeks with 1 to 2 level tablespoons of fertilizer.

Water

Water the tomato plants slowly and deeply to help them develop a strong root system. Do not let them wilt severely, or the yields and quality will be low.

Care

To increase your harvest, spread mulch around the tomato plants. Put a 2- to 3-inch layer of organic material such as compost, leaves, or hay around the growing plants. Mulching helps stop weed growth and water loss from the soil.

You can let tomatoes grow on the ground or support them with stakes or cages. If you stake the tomatoes, put the stake in shortly after transplanting to reduce root damage. A 6-foot-long stake set 10 inches deep in the soil works well.

As the plant grows taller, tie it loosely to the stake every 12 inches with pieces of rag or twine.

Source: rexhammock (CC BY-SA 2.0)

Square cages created to keep out squirrels

Source: SuperFantastic (CC BY 2.0)

Tomato plants that are caged don't need to be tied.

Prune the staked tomatoes to keep the vines manageable. Remove the small shoots that grow out of the point where each leaf joins the main stem by bending them sideways until they snap.

To develop the plant into two main vines, remove all but the lowest shoot. It will develop into a second branch.

Caging is another way to train tomato plants. You can make a good cage with a piece of concrete reinforcement wire 5 feet tall and 6 feet wide. Put the cages over the young plants. Push the cages down into the soil to keep them from blowing over.

Using this method, you can give the vine support without having to tie it.

To control weeds, you may cultivate or hoe around the plants. Work the soil only deep enough to kill the weeds but shallow enough not to damage the tomato plant roots.

Diseases

Many diseases as well as nematodes infect tomatoes in Texas, including anthracnose, bacterial leaf spot, blossom end rot, crown rot, damping-off, early blight, Fusarium wilt, late blight, leaf mold, Phytophthora blight, powdery mildew, root knot nematodes, southern blight, spotted wilt, tobacco mosaic, Verticillium wilt, and yellow leaf curl virus.

For more information, descriptions, control recommendations, and photos of common vegetable diseases, see the "Diseases" section starting on page 40.

Before using a pesticide, read the label and always follow cautions, warnings, and directions.

Insects

The most common insect pests are aphids, beet armyworms, flea beetles, cabbage loopers, Colorado potato beetles, corn earworms, cutworms, flea beetles, hornworms, leafminers, psyllids, stink bugs, and whiteflies.

Photographs, descriptions, and control recommendations for common vegetable insect pests are in the "Insects and other pests" section starting on page 61.

More information and photos on common tomato diseases and insect pests in Texas, see the Tomato Problem Solver at http://aggie-horticulture.tamu. edu/vegetable/problem-solvers/ tomato-problem-solver/.

Harvest

For best quality, pick tomatoes at full color. If you pick

Source: Source photon_de (CC BY 2.0)

Pick tomatoes at full color for best quality.

them when they are pink, let them ripen at room temperature. You can store them in the refrigerator after they reach full color.

Store

Place unripe tomatoes in a loosely closed paper bag at room temperature. Refrigerate ripe tomatoes in the crisper for no more than 2 or 3 days.

Cleanup

To reduce the potential for insect and disease problems next year, remove all the plant material and smooth the bed.

Zucchini and other squash

Best varieties for Texas

- **Acorn**
  Carnival
  Ebony
  Royal
  Table King
  Table Ace
  Table Queen
- **Butternut**
  Preclude II
  Waltham
- **Scallop**
  Early White Bush
  Patty Pan
  Peter Pan
  St. Patrick
  Starship
  Sunburst
- **Yellow**
  Burpee's Butterstick
  Dixie
  Early Prolific
  Early Summer
  Multipik
- **Zucchini**
  Ambassador
  Aristocrat
  Eight Ball Tigress
  El Dorado
  Goldfinger
  Gold Rush
  President
  Senator
  Sure Thing
  Tigress
  Zucchini Elite

Source: apple_pathways (CC BY 2.0)

Carnival acorn squash

Source: Mike Licht, NotionsCapital.com (CC BY 2.0)

Scallop squash

Source: smallfarmcentral_memberassembler (CC BY 2.0)

Butternut squash

Source: Mike Licht, Notions Capital.com (CC BY 2.0)

Yellow squash

Choose the site

Like most vining vegetables, squash grows best in sandy, fertile soils with a pH between 6.0 and 6.5.

Prep the soil

Remove all rocks and trash from the soil. Prepare it several weeks before planting, but only when the soil is dry enough not to stick to garden tools.

If possible, spread 2 to 3 inches of organic material such as compost, leaves, or rotted hay over the planting area. Then till to mix this organic material into the top 8 to 10 inches of soil.

Source: USDAgov (CC BY 2.0)

Zucchini

Source: randomduck (CC BY-SA 2.0)

Acorn squash

Source: RaeAllen (CC BY 2.0)

Mulched zucchini bed

Plant

Summer squash does not grow well in cool weather. Plant it in the spring after all danger of frost has passed.

For a good fall crop, plant early so the squash will mature before the first killing frost.

Plant the squash in hills 18 to 48 inches apart on rows 3 to 8 feet apart. The vining types, such as Hubbard or acorn, need more room than do the bush types.

Plant five or six seeds about 1 inch deep in each hill. Water after planting the seeds. After they sprout, thin them to three squash plants per hill.

Fertilize

Add 2 to 3 tablespoons of fertilizer such as 10-10-10 for each hill. Scatter the fertilizer evenly over a 2-foot by 2-foot area. Work it into the top 3 to 4 inches of soil.

When the first blooms appear, place about 2 tablespoons of garden fertilizer around each hill. Do not let the fertilizer touch the plants. Water the plants after fertilizing.

Water

Water the plants enough to keep them from wilting.

If the weather is really dry, water the squash at least once a week. Sandy soils need to be watered more often than heavy clay soils.

Care

Keep the squash plants free of weeds. Hoe around the plants to remove small weeds, being careful not to damage the

Source: Ruth and Dave (CC BY 2.0)

Squash varieties come in many colors, shapes, and sizes.

Source: thomas pix (CC BY 2.0)

Mulch helps protect zucchini and other squash from soil-borne diseases.

roots. Pull the weeds close to the plants by hand.

Diseases

Squash can get many diseases, especially when harvesting begins. To help control most diseases, spray the plants with an approved fungicide.

Common diseases of squash in Texas are Alternaria leaf spot, anthracnose, bacterial wilt, blossom-end rot, Choanephora wet rot, downy mildew, Fusarium wilt, mosaic, powdery mildew, silver leaf, squash leaf curl, and yellow vine.

For more information, descriptions, control recommendations, and photos of common vegetable diseases, see the "Diseases" section starting on page 40. Before using a pesticide, read the label and always follow cautions, warnings, and directions.

Insects

The most common insect pests are aphids, banded cucumber beetles, cabbage loopers, leafminers, spotted cucumber beetles, squash bugs, squash vine borers, and stink bugs.

Photographs, descriptions, and control recommendations for common vegetable insect pests are in the "Insects and other pests" section starting on page 61.

Harvest

Harvest summer squash when the fruit and seeds are small. Harvest yellow squash at 4 to 6 inches long; yellow

Source: davetoaster (CC BY 2.0)

Harvest summer squash when the seeds and fruit are small.

straight neck, 6 to 8 inches long. Harvest white scallops when they are 3 to 4 inches in diameter.

Always harvest mature squash so the plants will keep producing.

Harvest winter (hard rind) squash when they are full sized, the skin is hard, and the bottom of the fruit is a cream to orange color. A light frost will not damage fruits of winter squash.

Squash is best when cut, not pulled, from the vine.

Store

Store green and yellow squash in the refrigerator for about a week. Store winter squash for several months.

Cleanup

Add old squash vines to the compost pile or work them into the soil well before the spring planting season.

Herbs

Source: aldenchadwick (CC BY 2.0)

Herbs can grow in containers, in flowerbeds, as corner plantings, in rock gardens as borders, or in a special herb garden. Choose a sunny, well-drained location.

Some herbs are annuals, meaning that they grow from seeds and complete their life cycle in 1 year; some are biennial, which grow stems and leaves one year, grow flowers and fruits the second year, and then die; other herbs are perennials that return year after year.

Plant annual herbs in annual flower gardens or in vegetable gardens. Plant perennial herbs at the side of the garden where they will not interfere with next year's soil preparation.

Many gardeners establish a small herb garden near the

Choose a sunny location that drains well.

home. Generally, a 6- to 10-foot square or rectangular area is sufficient. You could also use a circular or freeform design.

Plant

For annual and biennial herbs, plant the seeds directly in the garden or start them indoors for later transplanting outside. Plant the tallest herbs at the back of the plot.

Propagate perennial herbs by division or by cuttings.

Division: Divide the plants every 3 or 4 years in the early spring. Dig up the plants and cut into several sections. Propagate chives and tarragon by dividing the roots or crowns.

Cuttings: Cut 4- to 6-inch sections of the stem, and root these by placing the cuttings in moist sand in a shady area. Roots should form on these cuttings in 4 to 8 weeks. Herbs such as sage and thyme can be propagated by cuttings.

Fertilize

Apply a balanced fertilizer but don't use too much nitrogen.

Water

Water the herbs as necessary during dry periods. Generally, add about 1 inch of water

Balcony herb garden

per week if it is not supplied by rainfall.

Because mints prefer moist soil, they must be watered often.

Care

Care for your herb garden as you would a vegetable or flower garden.

The most important factor affecting the normal growth and development of herbs is weeds. Keep the herbs weed-free all season. This is especially true for annual herbs and those that are small plants, not shrubs. Perennial herbs growing as small bushes can tolerate some weed pressure once they are established.

Mulch helps conserve soil moisture and reduces weed growth.

Diseases

In general, most herbs have few insect or disease problems. However, if a disease erupts, it is a more serious problem on herbs because the damage is already at a harmful stage once it becomes visible.

To reduce disease pressure, plant the herbs in suitable areas with proper air circulation and water drainage. Remove weak or infected leaves and other plant parts.

The most common diseases of herbs in Texas are leaf spots and powdery mildew. For information, descriptions, control recommendations, and photos of common plant diseases, see the "Diseases" section starting on page 40.

Before using a pesticide, read the label and always follow cautions, warnings, and directions.

Insects

Although most herbs tolerate minor infestations of feeding and chewing insects, do not allow the insect populations to explode.

Insects that damage herbs include aphids, flea beetles, leafhoppers, mites, thrips, weevils, and wireworms.

Plants outgrow insect feeding or damage if they are growing vigorously and are fertilized and watered properly. Harvest the herbs regularly to help keep insect pressure at a minimum.

Photographs, descriptions, and control recommendations for common vegetable insect pests are in the "Insects and other pests" section starting on page 61.

Harvest

For most herbs, gradually remove some of the leaves as needed, but do not remove all of them at one time. With proper care, the plants will produce over a long period.

Drying

After harvesting herbs, hang them in loosely tied bundles in a well-ventilated room. You could also spread the branches on a screen or cheesecloth, or spread the leaves on flat trays if you need only the leaves.

Source: thomas pix (CC BY 2.0)

When harvesting herbs, gradually remove some of the leaves you need—not all of them at once.

Source: Alex 'Skud' Bayley (CC BY 2.0)

Oregano drying

To keep dust off the herbs, cover them with a cloth or similar protective cover that allows moisture to pass through.

It is generally best to allow the herbs to dry naturally in a cool, dark room rather than to use artificial heat. You may lose flavor and quality by trying this drying method.

Store

Refrigerate unwashed fresh herbs in an open or perforated plastic bag and use them within 4 to 6 days.

Dried herbs

When the herbs are thoroughly dry, seal them in airtight containers such as fruit jars. Store them in a cool, dark location. Any sign of moisture accumulating in the jars indicates that the herbs are not thoroughly dry.

Pulverize the flower stalks

before putting them in jars. Store the leaves either pulverized or whole, depending on their intended use.

Store the seeds in labeled jars in a dark, cool, dry location. Some herb seeds, such as anise, caraway, coriander, or dill, can be used for flavoring.

Cleanup

To save your own seeds, harvest the entire seed head after it has dried on the plant. Then allow the seeds to dry in a cool, dry, protected location.

After the seeds are thoroughly dry, remove them from the heads and discard the trash.

Potted herbs

Some herbs can be planted in pots and grown indoors during the winter. Those best

Source: uberculture (CC BY 2.0)
Cliantro sprouts

adapted to pot culture are basil, chives, mint, parsley, rosemary, and sweet marjoram.

You could either start these herbs from seeds indoors or dig them up from the garden toward the end of the growing season and place them in pots.

Set them in a sunny south window, and care for them as you would houseplants.

Source: John E. Colvin
Sage, cilantro, oregano, rosemary, thyme, and parsley growing in a window

Edible herbs suitable for growing in Texas

Annual and biennial herbs

Annuals grow from seeds and complete their life cycle in 1 year. They will be killed by frost and must be started from seed each year. Biennials grow stems and leaves the first year and produce flowers, fruits, and seeds the second year.

Sourcezzz: Bill Watson

Anise leaves

Anise

Annual

Height: 20 to 24 inches

Site selection/planting/care: Moderately rich soil; likes full sun; space 3 to 4 inches within the row with the rows 12 to 14 inches apart

Harvest: When the seeds turn brown, or use the leaves as needed while green

---

Source: Jerrold Summerlin

Basil

Annual

Height: 20 to 24 inches

Site selection/planting/care: Trim often to keep the plants bushy; space 12 inches apart; prefers protected sun, well-drained soils, and raised beds

Harvest: When flowering begins; cut plants 4 to 6 inches above ground

Caraway

Caraway seeds

Annual or biennial

Height: 12 to 24 inches

Site selection/planting/care: Seed directly in spring in full sun; space 6 inches apart; some cultivars are annuals

Harvest: Mature leaves; seeds will form midway through the second season

Cilantro/coriander

Source: Bill Watson

Annual

Height: 36 inches

Site selection/planting/care: Sow seeds directly in full sun or partial shade; thin to 10 inches apart

Harvest: Mature seed heads before the seeds drop; leaves when they are small

Dill

Source: Jerrold Summerlin

Annual

Height: 24 to 36 inches

Site selection/planting/care: Seed in sun or partial shade; thin to 12 inches apart; if the seeds mature and fall, the plants will return the next year

Harvest: When the seeds turn brown, or use the leaves as needed while green

Source: Bill Watson

Fennel bulb and leaves

Fennel

Annual or perennial

Height: 36 inches

Site selection/planting/care: Seed in early spring and thin to 12 inches apart

Harvest: Leaves when flowering begins; harvest young sprigs, leaves, or seeds; bulbs when mature, usually in the spring

---

Source: Jerrold Summerlin

Flat leaf Italian parsley

Parsley *(flat leaf Italian or curly)*

Biennial

Height: 5 to 6 inches

Site selection/planting/care: Seed in early spring in full sun; germinates slowly; space 6 to 8 inches apart; transplants are easier to grow

Harvest: Mature leaves as needed

Source: Karelj (CC BY-SA 3.0 or GFDL)

Summer savory

Annual

Height: 12 to 18 inches

Site selection/planting/care: Well-drained, sandy to loamy soil; prefers full sun; sow seed in early spring; space or thin to 10 inches apart

Harvest: Leafy tops when plants start to show buds

Perennial herbs

These grow from seed; some are propagated by other means. Generally the top part of the plant dies in the winter and regrows from the roots the following spring. Protect perennials from cold damage.

Source: Bill Watson

Bay

Height: Tree, 10 feet tall; leaves, 1 to 4 inches long

Site selection/planting/care: Bay is difficult to propagate from seeds or cuttings. Grows well in pots.; needs full sun and well-draining soil

Harvest: Mature leaves as needed

Source: Jerrold Summerlin

Chives

Height: 12 inches

Site selection/planting/care: Can be grown in containers or outdoors in spring in sun or partial shade; divide to increase; space 5 inches apart

Harvest: Leaves as needed

Source: Bill Watson

Mint *(peppermint or spearmint)*

Height: 18 to 36 inches

Site selection/planting/care: Prefers rich, moist soil; full sun or partial shade; space 8 to 10 inches apart

Harvest: Young or mature leaves

Source: Jerrold Summerlin

Oregano

Height: 24 inches

Site selection/planting/care: Plant in rich soil in full sun; space 8 to 10 inches apart

Harvest: Mature leaves

Source: Bill Watson

Rosemary

Height: 30 to 60 inches

Site selection/planting/care: Start cuttings in early spring in full sun; seeds germinate slowly; space 24 inches apart

Harvest: Mature leaves; clip the tops when the plants are in full bloom

Source: Jerrold Summerlin

Sage

Height: 18 to 36 inches

Site selection/planting/care: Plant in a well-drained location; full sun; seeds germinate slowly; space 30 inches apart

Harvest: Leaves when flowering begins

Marjoram, sweet

Height: 8 to 12 inches

Site selection/planting/care: Start seedlings in shade; mature plants will grow in full sun; space 8 to 10 inches apart

Harvest: Leaves when flowering begins

Source: Bill Watson

Tarragon *(select French tarragon)*

Height: 24 inches

Site selection/planting/care: Prefers well-drained soils, full sun; grow from divisions or root cuttings; space 12 inches apart

Harvest: Leaves when flowering begins

Source: Jerrold Summerlin

Thyme

Height: 8 to 12 inches

Site selection/planting/care: Start seeds indoors; prefers full sun and well-drained soils; space 10 to 12 inches apart

Harvest: Leaves and flower clusters before the first flowers open; clip the tops when the plants are in full bloom

Index

East Texas

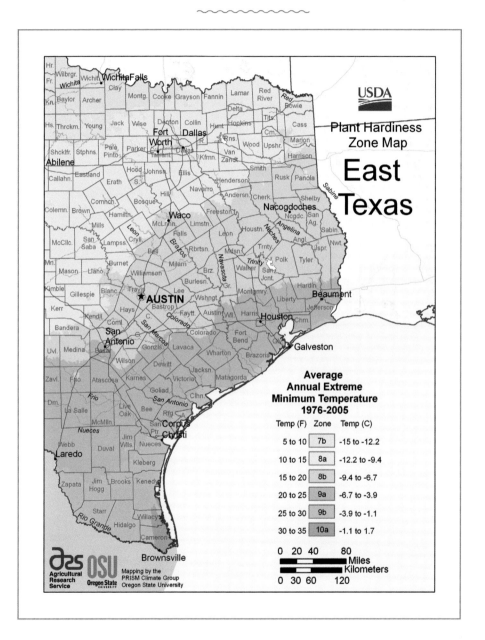

West Texas

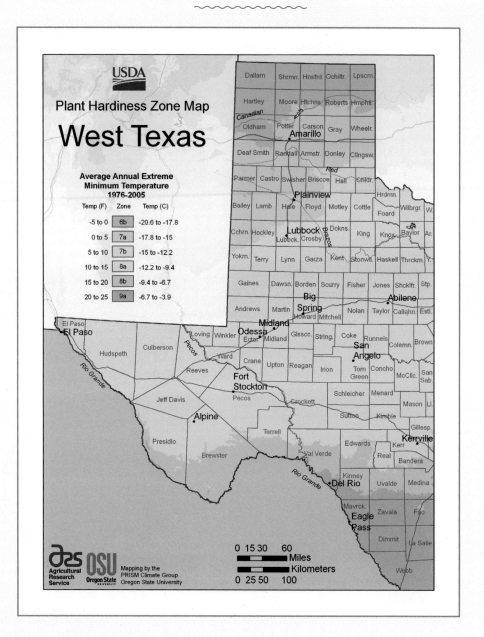